GunControl=People Control

by

William R. Tonso

authorHOUSE

1663 LIBERTY DRIVE, SUITE 200
BLOOMINGTON, INDIANA 47403
(800) 839-8640
www.authorhouse.com

First published by AuthorHouse 06/29/04

ISBN: 1-4184-1496-4 (e-book)
ISBN: 1-4184-1497-2 (Paperback)

Library of Congress Control Number: 2004090072

This book is printed on acid free paper.

Printed in the United States of America
Bloomington, IN

To Beverley, my beautiful wife and editor.

Table of Contents

INTRODUCTION

The eleven of my essays that I've assembled for this book on various aspects of the gun issue have all been published previously, the earliest in 1985, the most recent in 2003, and eight of them have been reprinted at least once in other publications. Sometime back it occurred to me that taken together and arranged properly, not merely according to publication date, these particular essays sort of flow one to the next and rather neatly link media, popular cultural, and people-control aspects of the gun issue regularly ignored by the mainstream media and only rarely examined by academic scholars. So that's what I've tried to do. The media essays deal with the nature of anti-gun bias in the mainstream media, and attempt to explain it. The popular culture essays examine changes in the popular-cultural treatments of guns and their users over the past three-plus decades, and consider the social impact of these changes. The people-control chapters get into the deep politics of gun control, not just the conflict between the National Rifle Association and the gun prohibitionists, but what the latter are actually trying to accomplish. Then there are a couple of spoof pieces. I suspect that not only Second Amendment supporters, but libertarians and conservatives in general and maybe even some liberals will find all this interesting. But before I say any more about these essays, I'd like to explain to the reader how I acquired the perspective and motivation that prompted me to write them.

For twenty-nine of my seventy years I made my living as a sociology professor, and that's how and where I acquired my perspective. But I've been immersed in the

American gun culture from the day I was born, and the gun-prohibitionist attempt to demonize our gun culture has provided my motivation. One of my earliest memories, dating back to before my fourth birthday, was of guns in a family context: my dad oiling pistols he then owned—a couple or three Colt semiautomatics that he kept in the boxes in which they came. Guns remained an everyday part of my life during my childhood and youth, all kinds of guns—cap pistols, water pistols, cork-launching guns, suction-cup-dart guns, homemade inner-tube-rubber-band-launching guns (with which my neighborhood friends and I had running battles in those pre-paintball days), rubber-band-powered BB guns, airguns, and real firearms. When I was still very young, I knew where the loaded house gun, a big 1917 Colt .45 revolver, was kept in my folks' bedroom. The other guns and ammunition for them were kept in a locked closet in my bedroom, and I knew where the key to that closet was kept. But I never once even considered touching any of those guns without permission from and supervision by my dad.

I was hooked on guns from my earliest days, therefore, not as a hunter or formal target shooter, though I've done some of the latter, but as a plinker and general enthusiast. In my home town, Herrin, Illinois (then still primarily a coal-mining community) located in the far south of the state, the part of the state with hills and trees and no big cities, guns were common. Though Herrin had been a wild place a few years before I was born, with violent conflicts between mine labor and management, the Ku Klux Klan and those who opposed it, and rival gangs violating Prohibition, it was very peaceful by the time I came along. It was common to see people on their way to hunting or shooting sessions in the country carrying guns down the street, my dad, mom, and

I among them from the time I was big enough to walk the distance. One of my maternal aunt's brothers-in-law was a local gunsmith. All of my older male relatives and most of their close male friends owned guns, and I spent a lot of time talking to my dad about guns as he collected more of them over the years and I started accumulating them. Except for "Superman" and the other superheroes of those days (who didn't interest me much), all of the popular-cultural heroes whose adventures were set during the age of firearms carried guns and were skilled in their use. Our soldiers in the movie newsreels used guns. I read about guns in gun, outdoor, and men's magazines such as *True* and *Argosy*. I picked up an interest in drawing early on, and on rainy days I'd sit for long spells and draw guns (and airplanes and soldiers), either trying to copy them accurately from photographs or drawings in magazines or catalogs or designing my own. I never heard anti-gun sentiments expressed in those days.

When the first federal gun laws, the National Firearms Act and the Federal Firearms Act, were enacted in 1934 and 1938 respectively, I was too young for them to make an impression on me. On December 7, 1941, less than two-and-a-half months after my eighth birthday, the world outside of my hometown made its first impression on me that I can date—I remember the radio report of the Japanese attack on Pearl Harbor. World War II put an end to national concerns about gun control just at the time that my awareness was being expanded. Consequently, I grew up completely unaware that there ever had been such concerns in the United States.

During WWII, and even through the Korean War, gun use by loyal Americans and our allies was celebrated through the entertainment as well as the news media. When my dad joined the National Rifle Association (NRA) in the late 1940s, I viewed it as no more than a subscription to that organization's magazine, the *American Rifleman.* A friend of his had previously been an NRA member, and he would pass his magazines on to us when he finished reading them. I suspect that part of the reason that my dad joined was to facilitate receiving a surplus WWI 1917 Enfield rifle through the Army's Office of the Director of Civilian Marksmanship. I became an NRA member in 1955, because I was on the Southern Illinois University (SIU) Air Force Reserve Officers Training Corps rifle team, which was affiliated with the NRA. Neither my dad nor I joined for political reasons, because there were no political reasons of which we were aware for joining in those days. In fact, I considered my membership to be something of a waste since we already were receiving the *Rifleman* at home.

During the late 1950s, the gun-control movement that had lain dormant and out of my awareness for about two decades started to stir enough to get my attention, though my memory of specific events is vague—a Gallup poll claiming that Americans supported a ban on handguns here, an uninformed comment on gun ownership there. But by the early 1960s it was keeping my attention with the push to ban "Saturday night specials." As that decade became ever more turbulent with its assassinations and riots, the mainstream media (entertainment as well as news) bombarded the nation with demands for ever more restrictive controls on the civilian possession of guns, and I became ever more aggravated with these media as well as at the movers and shakers of the anti-gun movement. The pattern was set. The movers and shakers would spout what to me were the most ludicrous claims about guns and/or their use in the United States, and the mainstream media would uncritically pass those claims on to the public. Example: Cheap "Saturday night specials" are deadly in the bands of criminals, but completely useless to honest folks trying to protect themselves against criminals. Say what?! But what aggravated me even more was that guns and the literally tens of millions of peaceful people like me and my dad who were interested in them were being blamed for the nation's violence problems, and the call was for restricting *our* access to guns. Yet we weren't allowed anywhere near equal mainstream media access to the public to respond to this demonization and to oppose these restrictions. Those sneering politicos, news anchors, editorialists, and columnists who to me demonstrated their incredible ignorance and/or downright dishonesty with every word they uttered about guns and gun owners were sneering at me and mine and at interests that I had never had reason to believe were anything but wholesome and honorable.

Fast forward a couple of decades from the middle 1950s, during which time I received my bachelor's degree in something called industrial education from SIU, along with a commission as a second lieutenant; served three years' active duty in the USAF, mostly as a ground control radar interceptor director and senior director of radar crews in the North American Air Defense Command; worked white collar in industry and as a supervisor of the handicapped in a closed workshop; earned a master's degree in business administration specializing in personnel management from SIU; started professing sociology at the University of Evansville in Indiana; got married; and finished my doctorate in sociology at SIU. It was my dissertation, which benefited tremendously from my immersion in my professing specialties, the sociology of deviance, minority and ethnic group relations, and social theory, that started me writing about the social and cultural aspects of the gun issue. Published as *Gun and Society: The Social and Existential Roots of the American Attachment to Firearms* in 1982, it examined the social settings in which guns were developed, how they were used (practically, recreationally, and symbolically), who encouraged or discouraged their use by whom, *and how their efforts were related to the control of others,* from the time guns came on the scene in Europe in the 14th century to contemporary times. To the extent that my work is accepted it undermines much of the gun prohibitionists' position; however, its purpose was to shed scholarly light on the roots of the interest in guns here and elsewhere, not to oppose controls. Similarly, my 1990 edited book, *The Gun Culture and Its Enemies,* which includes a couple of chapters by me, attempted to shed light on the social and cultural roots of the conflict over guns.

Before I started professing sociology, I came to believe that it's very important for social and behavioral scientists to separate as much as possible their roles as scientists or scholars from their everyday private-citizen roles. I had become an extreme relativist and social constructionist; but as I reminded my students over the years, while I think that relativism is an indispensable tool for social scientists, it provides us with no principle to live by day to day. To me as a sociologist, moral right and wrong and even "truth" as we know it, are socially constructed and relative and subject to social scientific exploration, but in my everyday interaction with others I don't treat moral right and wrong and truth that way. In the everyday world we have to be judgmental, but as social scientists charged with trying to figure out what others are doing in the world around us, if we don't do our best to avoid judging those whom we're studying we produce propaganda under the guise of research findings arrived at through the application of a supposedly neutral and objective scientific method. I've dealt with this issue in some detail in "Social Problems and Sagecraft: Gun Control as a Case in Point," a paper on anti-gun bias in college sociology textbooks that received quite a bit of publicity, thanks to the well-known Second Amendment scholar and pro-gun writer Don B. Kates, Jr. It is included in his 1984 book *Firearms and Violence: Issues of Public Policy* and, slightly revised, in a special 1983 issue of *Law & Policy Quarterly* that he edited. It also appears in Lee Nisbet's *The Gun Control Debate: You Decide.*

But while I became quite capable of standing back and taking a detached look at the controversial gun issue in relativistic terms for sociological purposes—no right or wrong side, just different and competing sides—I've never forgotten which side of the issue I'm on and why I'm on it. And the sneering politicos, news anchors, editorialists, and columnists still aggravate me in everyday-judgment-passing life, even though I understand where they're coming from. Understanding in a sociologically-detached manner why people are as they are doesn't necessarily encourage condoning the way they are. So over the years, I've not only tried to shed light on the gun controversy in a detached manner through a few of my sociological writings, but responded in kind to the gun prohibitionists through a number of critiques of their movement. And I readily acknowledge that when dealing with controversial social phenomena such as the gun issue, the line between the analytical and the critical is subjectively fuzzy. Is exploring the obvious people-control agenda the gun prohibitionists never acknowledge analysis or criticism?

My often sociologically-informed, but unabashedly anti-gun-control-movement writings over the past two-and-a-half decades have ranged from the hundred-plus letters and a few columns published in local newspapers, to columns and articles in such publications as *The Quill,* the magazine of Sigma Delta Chi, the Society of Professional Journalists, the Law Enforcement Association of America's *Advocate, Reason, Liberty, Chronicles, The American Legion Magazine, American Rifleman, American Hunter, Gun Week, Gun News Digest, Outdoor Life, USA Today, The Baltimore Sun, The Cleveland Plain Dealer,* and *The Washington Times.*

The eleven essays in this book originally appeared in either *Chronicles, Gun Week, Liberty,* or *Reason.* They're taken from my original manuscripts rather than the editorially-altered published versions, and I've used my original titles rather than those of the published pieces when the latter have been different from mine. One essay has been updated, but the rest have not. Consequently, *statistics cited in a given essay, for example, are those available at the time it was written, and they may differ from those cited in essays written years before or after it was written.* In some cases, I've altered my originals to avoid repetition, but the reader will still find quotes from the founding generation concerning the meaning of the Second Amendment in more than one essay and a few other repeats that I felt that I couldn't remove without leaving a gap in an essay. Each essay was, after all, written to stand alone, and not as I'm using them here, to lead into the next essay as chapters lead from one to the next in standard books. Some essays are written less formally than others in that I use contractions in them. At the beginning of each essay, I've provided a brief italicized publishing history for it. The three essays in Part I all deal with the mainstream media treatment of the gun issue, the two in part II deal with the treatment of guns in the popular culture and its impact, the four in Part III deal with the people-control agenda of the gun prohibitionists and reasons for opposing it, and the two in Part IV spoof the people-control efforts of the prohibitionists. The essays need not be read in this order, however, since as I've mentioned, each stands on its own.

Back in 1984, there were a number of mainstream media commentaries celebrating what their authors considered to be the fact that the media-assisted totalitarian world described by George Orwell in his novel *1984* had not come to pass. Maybe not, but as an informed opponent of gun controls, to me there was (and still is) much Orwellian about the mainstream media treatment of the gun issue. I made my case in "Guns, the Media, and 1984," which was originally published as "Calling the Shots" in the March, 1985 issue of the libertarian magazine *Reason*. It was the recipient of a Second Amendment Foundation *James Madison Award* "For excellence in Journalism promoting the Individual Right to Keep and Bear Arms." In this essay, I argue, as former CBS reporter Bernard Goldberg did in his book *Bias* eighteen years later, that much media bias is rooted in the unexamined assumptions that media gatekeepers carry into their examination of the world around them. Though the examples are dated, they're worth revisiting, and the analysis still holds. "Big Journalism's War On the Second Amendment" was originally published as "Shooting Blind" in the November, 1995 issue of *Reason*. It focuses on the mainstream-media treatment of the "assault weapon" issue, and it even notes a misleading CBS documentary contribution by now media critic Goldberg, and cites evidence that the mainstream media treatment of the gun issue can go beyond ignorance and unexamined assumptions to chicanery. My original manuscripts of these two articles herein presented are somewhat different from the published versions. "The Most Dangerous Amendment" was originally published in the December, 1999 issue of the paleoconservative magazine *Chronicles*. In it, I argue that the abuse of First Amendment rights by the mainstream entertainment as well as news media causes far more social damage than does the abuse of Second Amendment rights by the populace at large. In fact, the case can be made that by pushing their First Amendment rights to the limits, the mainstream news and entertainment media unintentionally foster the abuse of Second Amendment rights.

The last article in the Part I on the media and guns, segues into Part II on popular culture and guns, the first essay of which is "Hollywood and the Meaning of Guns." It was originally published as "Guns and the Movies" in the October, 2000 issue of the libertarian magazine *Liberty*. This essay takes on the entertainment industry's position that widespread gun ownership in the United States rather than the industry's movies and other products is responsible for our violence problems. It also comments on the shift in the popular-cultural treatment of guns that has occurred since the 1960s, and the possible social impact of that shift. The other essay in this part, "Sundays Past: Guns, Popular Culture, Family, and Me," is primarily a nostalgic reminiscence dealing with the intertwined impact guns, popular culture, and family had on me as a child in my small hometown back in the 1930s and 1940s, but it also contains some social criticism and is sort of a personalized extension of the "Hollywood" essay. It was published originally as "Sundays Past" in the December, 2001 issue of *Liberty*. This is the only essay presented herein that has been updated, and its critique of popular culture segues into Part III of the book on people control and guns.

Toward the end of "Sundays Past," I lament the passing of the old popular-cultural heroes, and the tendency of today's society to breed underclass thugs and urban, middle-class wimps. The first essay of Part III elaborates on this theme. "The Spirit of Northfield and Coffeyville," was published in the October, 2000 issue of *Liberty*. Those familiar with the history of the Wild West will recognize the names of these two communities. The citizens of the former wiped out the James/Younger gang in 1876, while those of the latter wiped out the Dalton gang in 1892. Now self-help is discouraged, while we're encouraged to rely on the armed agents of government to protect us, and even minorities seem unaware that these government agents can pose a far greater threat to us than do common street thugs. "Racism, Elitism, and Gun Control," published originally as "Gun Control: White Man's Law" in the December, 1985 issue of *Reason,* picks up on this theme. In a letter response to *Reason's* version of this essay, I was criticized for implying that the people-control aspects of gun controls are primarily rooted in racism. As should be clear from my original title and my original manuscript presented herein, I meant to imply no such thing. The third essay of Part III, "Gun Control and Elites of the Right and Left," published as "Guns and the Ruling Elite" in the September, 1996 issue of *Liberty,* makes clear my position on the people-control aspects of gun control. The gun prohibitionists and their media allies would have us believe that the politics of the gun issue go no deeper than the tactics the NRA uses to defeat what the prohibitionist claim is needed legislation. People control, of course, can't be acknowledged. The final essay of Part III, "Assault Weapons Again?," published in the September/October, 2003 issue of *Liberty* as "All Guns to the People," emphasizes that the Founders intended that we be armed as a guard against tyranny, and that until relatively recently no one questioned our right to possess military firearms or guns with more power and/or firepower than those carried by common soldiers.

Both of the short essays of Part IV, "How About Car Control?" and "Guns and Superstition: Then and Now," were published in *Gun Week* in 1988, September 30 and June 10, respectively. Both spoof specific efforts of the gun prohibitionists—"Car Control," the effort to ban "Saturday night specials," and "Superstition," the effort to equate gun control with disease control.

From these eleven essays, it should be obvious that I see gun control as an effort on the part of various elites, sometimes in conjunction with each other, primarily to control people rather than to control crime. As I demonstrate through these essays, ethnic elites have attempted to keep ethnic minorities and immigrants in line by restricting their access to guns; business elites on the right have so attempted to keep labor in line; and modern, urban-oriented, cosmopolitan elites on the left have so attempted to contain rural- and small-town-oriented, bedrock traditionalists on the right who are unwilling to cooperate with their social engineering efforts. As I also demonstrate, the cosmopolitan elites have been able to make the gun issue part of the cultural war they're waging against bedrock America on many fronts. They've done this by demonizing guns and deviantizing gun ownership through their mainstream-media propaganda arm in an attempt to convince Americans that they shouldn't own guns. The sociological side of me brings these elite people-control efforts and class, ethnic, and cultural conflicts to my attention, but it's my bedrock gun-culture roots that make me a no-compromise opponent of the cosmopolitan social-engineering agenda—that and the distrust I have of those "coercive utopians" who regularly try to circumvent our constitutional safeguards in what they would have us believe are selfless efforts to promote the public interest. The "war on terrorism" gives them more cover for their attempts to circumvent the Constitution. So now the reader knows how I acquired the perspective and motivation that prompted me to write these essays.

In September, 2004, the clearly unconstitutional and ludicrous Clinton-administration ban on oxymoronic "semiautomatic assault weapons" (semiautomatics aren't assault anything) and magazines capable of holding over ten cartridges is scheduled to sunset. The gun prohibitionists and their allies in the mainstream media are already marshaling their forces in an effort to extend and expand these bans or to make them permanent. I hope that this collection of essays can play a part in combating their efforts. In fact, I've chosen the self-publishing route with AuthorHouse because it will ensure that my book becomes available several months before these bans are scheduled to expire *sans* Congressional action to save them from such a fate. Thanks to those original publishers who hold the rights to some of the following essays for permission to republish them here.

I dedicated my first book, *Gun and Society,* to my parents, Eva and Joe Tonso, or Mater and Pater, as I started calling them back in my smart-alecky undergraduate days. I can't imagine better parents, and I hope that "Sundays Past" provides the reader with some idea of why I feel this way. I dedicated my edited second book, *The Gun Culture and Its Enemies,* to them again, my wife Beverley, and my fellow contributors. This book, I dedicate to Beverley, my beautiful wife and editor, by herself. Nothing that I write leaves the house without her stamp of approval, which means that she's read a lot more about the gun issue than she's cared to read. It isn't that she disagrees with me, but it's not a burning issue with her and she's very appreciative when I write on other topics—any other topics! Thanks, Chirp!

PART I:

GUNS AND MEDIA BIAS

GUNS, THE MEDIA, AND 1984

Original manuscript of an essay first published as "Calling the Shots" in Reason, *March, 1985, and reprinted in the Second Amendment Foundation's Monograph Series, 1986. It received SAF's James Madison Award "For excellence in Journalism promoting the Individual Right to Keep and Bear Arms."*

An article entitled "The Demography of Gun Control" appeared in the September 20, 1975 issue of *The Nation*. Its author was University of Massachusetts at Amherst sociologist James D. Wright, and the article's tone was rather urgent. According to Wright, the United States has far and away the most heavily armed civilian population in history, and as a result this country has the dubious distinction of topping all other industrial nations in injury and death resulting from crime. Therefore, the United States badly needs tougher gun controls—controls that the vast majority of Americans, even the majority of those who own guns, favor, according to the public opinion polls. Classic mainstream-media fare on guns, but this time by someone with impressive social scientific credentials.

Why have gun controls not been enacted? According to Wright, the National Rifle Association, the powerful "gun lobby" representing the hard-core, anti-control minority among gun owners, has been able to thwart efforts to enact such measures. Therefore, if this opposition is to be overcome, it must be understood and controls should be designed, if at all possible, to take the NRA's interests into consideration. But an effort must be made to keep this relatively small, unrepresentative minority from subverting democratic processes. "Those 23,000 people who will otherwise be accidentally shot next year, not to mention the 8,000 who will intentionally be shot to death, will no doubt be grateful."

Wright also took the preceding position on gun control in a manner somewhat less urgent and openly polemical and more in keeping with the expectations of a scholarly audience, in "The Ownership of the Means of Destruction," an article in the October 1975 issue of *Social Problems* that he co-authored with sociologist Linda Marston. This article was a standard scholarly treatment of the gun issue at the time. But then in 1978, the National Institute of Justice (NIJ) presented the U of M's Social and Demographic Research Institute with a grant to examine critically all of the scholarly literature that could be found on the gun issue with the object of determining what reasonably could be accepted and what could not be supported concerning the link between guns and crime. Wright and his U of M colleague, Peter H. Rossi, both of whom are specialists in social scientific methods, set out to accomplish this task.

Wright and Rossi's critical review of gun control scholarship took three years to complete, and in 1981 it was published by NIJ and distributed by the U.S. Government Printing Office under the title *Weapons, Crime and Violence in America: A Literature Review and Research Agenda.* Two years later in 1983, Aldine Publishing Company released a slightly revised and updated version of this study under the title *Under the Gun: Weapons, Crime, and Violence in America.* So what did Wright, Rossi, and Kathleen Daly, a State University of New York at Albany sociologist who is a third co-author of the Aldine edition of the book, conclude as a result of their meticulous critical review? They found, to their surprise, that most gun control studies including those federal and otherwise regularly cited to justify the enactment of stricter gun controls, were very politicized and extremely poorly done. However, sifting through the volumes of previous studies trying to separate findings that seemed to have been adequately supported through research from those that did not seem to have been supported, Wright and company reached such specific conclusions as the following: (1) though there are millions of guns in civilian hands in the United States, there is reason to believe that there are tens of millions fewer than are generally claimed both by those who support stricter gun controls and by those who oppose them; (2) there is little reason to believe that Americans are engaged in a domestic arms race of significant proportions brought on by their fear of street crime, militant minorities, the breakdown of law and order, and general civil disorder; (3) evidence to the effect that widespread gun ownership is either a cause, effect, or deterrent of crime is inconclusive; (4) while approximately two thirds of all gun crimes in this country involve handguns (no crime cause implied), there is no conclusive proof (partly due to definitional problems) that "Saturday night specials" are more likely to be used criminally than are other handguns, about half of which are acquired for sporting purposes; (5) while there is widespread public support for gun controls, the kinds of controls widely supported are no more restrictive than those regulating the ownership of automobiles and other "intrinsically dangerous objects"—in other words, there is little support for handgun bans, or for undue restrictions on gun ownership; (6) for various reasons, there is little evidence to suggest that existing gun laws have reduced violent crime appreciably, if at all; and finally, (7) "the prospects for ameliorating the problem of criminal violence through stricter controls over civilian ownership, purchase, or use of firearms are dim."

As Wright's articles in *The Nation* and in *Social Problems* indicate, and as he acknowledges in *Under the Gun,* he began this study accepting "the progressive's indictment of American firearms policy"—and Rossi had shared his views. But as they write in *Under the Gun,* "The more deeply we have explored the empirical implications of this indictment, the less plausible it has become." Incredible! Wright, the author of pro-control articles that have appeared in prestigious national publications, an established sociologist with six books and some fifty scholarly articles and papers to his credit, and Rossi, a past president of the American Sociological Association with 20 books and over 125 articles and papers to his credit, *as a result of their critical exploration of the literature on the subject,* have both backed away from the pro-gun-control position that is part and parcel of the conventional wisdom of the intellectual establishment of which they are both a part. Such a shift in position on gun control in intellectual circles is unprecedented. And given the caliber of the researchers involved and the fact that their findings undermine almost all of the information on gun control regularly disseminated through the major media, it would seem that there is an important story in all of this if the objective of the media, as stated *ad nauseam* through various lofty mottoes, is to keep the public informed. So much for lofty mottoes.

On November 17,1981, one of our two daily newspapers here in Evansville, Indiana carried a brief United Press report on the findings of the NIJ study under the head "Gun Study Results are Inconclusive." The article was stuck back on page four and it summed up so much in less than 250 words that little sense could be made out of the study's findings. Within a few days of this newspaper report, I happened to be watching one of the evening national news broadcasts when brief mention was made of the NIJ study. The TV newsman dismissed this thorough work with a scoffing comment to the effect that he could not imagine how the gun-crime link could be questioned. The only mention of this study in our other daily paper, as far as I am aware, came through a letter of mine to the editor in January of 1984. Since the release of the NIJ findings, the total number of major and local media treatments of the gun issue (news reports, editorials, columns, and TV specials) that I have read or watched runs into the hundreds, but of these, only public television's 1983 *Frontline* offering, "Gunfight U.S.A.," has reflected any familiarity with the work of Wright and his colleagues. Wright, in fact, was one of several gun control "authorities" interviewed for "Gunfight U.S.A.," and it may be significant that this *Frontline* segment is one of the very rare major media treatments of the gun control issue that has questioned the utility and desirability of such measures.

If the pattern that I have observed locally holds for the rest of the nation, it appears that after an initial tiny splash of acknowledgment through some major and lesser urban newspapers and the TV networks, the NIJ study has hardly created a ripple in the standard overwhelmingly pro-control major media coverage of the gun issue. A phone call to Wright, whom I had met briefly when we both took part in a symposium on the gun issue in Washington, D.C. in 1981, did nothing to dispel this conclusion. When I asked Wright how his book, *Under the Gun*, had been received by the major media, he indicated that with a few exceptions, the most prestigious being *The San Francisco Chronicle*, it had been ignored, even though review copies had been sent to all of the major urban newspapers and to the news and intellectual magazines that regularly review books, and I might add, regularly support gun controls. It appears, therefore, that there is a very good chance that the great majority of the Americans who are exposed to the gun control controversy exclusively through the major and lesser urban media (newspapers, news and general interest magazines, and the TV networks) have never heard of, or know very little about, a thorough study conducted by reputable social scientists that calls into question almost everything that these media disseminate regularly concerning the gun issue. As a long-time follower of the treatment that the gun issue has received through these media, none of the preceding surprises me.

As I acknowledged in an article entitled "Media Culture and Guns" that appeared in the March 1983 issue of *The Quill,* the major media shutout of information and arguments that tend to call into question the desirability of gun controls of the sort that would severely restrict, or make possible the severe restriction of, the possession of guns commonly owned by American citizens has not been complete. In fact, major media dissemination of the views of the critics of such controls seems to have improved significantly since the late 1970s as exemplified by public TV's "Gunfight U.S.A.," several editions of *Crossfire*, and anti-control or reasonably balanced articles and columns in such publications as *The New York Times* and other major urban newspapers, *Harper's, Commonweal, Penthouse, Playboy, Esquire, Glamour*, and *New Woman*. Yet the major media have a long way to go before their coverage of the gun issue could be considered adequate as far as even-handed reportage of information, arguments, and developments is concerned. Pro-control information and arguments get 37 inches of print to every anti-control inch in the print media, and more than 7 minutes to every minute in the electronic media, according to one of the anti-control organizations. And there is still a certain tokenism about the media's occasional presentation of information and arguments that tend to undermine the pro-control effort, in that such information and arguments, with few exceptions, seem to have little impact upon the everyday major media editorializing and reporting on the gun issue. Why?

Syndicated columnist Russell Baker has written recently that "The American press is a stuffed-shirt institution, overbearing in its earnestness, much given to sober self-examination of the self-congratulatory variety." During the course of one such self-congratulatory self-examination conducted a few years ago by Eric Sevaried, George Will, Tom Wicker, and Ben Wattenberg, Sevaried commented, "I used to get all kinds of letters and telegrams from people—sometimes very angry people. When they accused me of bias, it usually was because they disagreed with the substance of something I had said. It never occurred to them that they might be biased." To which Wattenberg replied that the issue was not necessarily one of deliberate media bias or conspiracy. "The question is, do the people who make up the elites of the press corps in New York and Washington—on the networks, in the syndicated columns, and so forth—tend to see the same reality that the rest of the country sees?" Provincial media folk who take the urban elite as their model could be added to Wattenberg's list.

Sevaried's comment and Wattenberg's response, the point of which apparently did not register with his colleagues since they ignored him, are reminiscent of an exchange I had with a critic of my article in *The Quill*. Though crediting the media with slightly better-balanced coverage of the gun issue in recent years, my article pointed out that the major media have been and still are heavily permeated by a pro-gun-control bias, and a journalism professor took issue with my claim. Following Sevaried's line of reasoning, this academic suggested that I saw the media as biased because they failed to reflect my own anti-gun-control bias. Then, in a personal letter to me, he stated further that issues are covered in the media "according to the merits of the various positions as judged by editors and broadcast news directors." I replied that I did not doubt that editors and broadcast news directors generally try to weigh such matters when they are making their decisions, but "I do claim that when these judgments are made in accordance with 'cosmopolitan' world views, values, and ignorance concerning gun-related matters, etc., a pro-control orientation permeates the major media treatment (entertainment as well as news) of the gun issue so thoroughly that the public is generally misled or uninformed about many matters of importance related to this issue." I suspect that Wattenberg might understand, but I doubt that the professor did or that Sevaried or many other media folk would, so I will explain further.

The standard media treatment of the gun issue is based on three unquestioned or even unquestionable assumptions that coincide with the articles of faith of the pro-control organizations and facilitate the ready acceptance of the news releases of these organizations as informed and factual, and the rejection of opposing information as biased: (1) guns, especially handguns, are troublesome unto themselves, apart from the people who misuse them; therefore, (2) all reasonable and informed Americans want to do something about the "gun problem" as (3) other modern, urban, industrial nations have done through gun controls. These assumptions affect news coverage and commentaries directly, because they provide reporters, editors, columnists, and broadcast news directors with themes to build stories and editorials around; e.g., "here is another case of gun crime," or "here is another case of responsible citizens trying to do something about gun crime," or "here is another case of the 'gun lobby' blocking needed gun legislation." Problems arise, however, when potentially reportable events, situations, or conditions are not readily interpreted in terms of these three unquestioned assumptions or articles of faith. The release of the findings of the NIJ study produced one such anomaly, and countless others come to mind.

If guns are troublesome unto themselves, how is a study that criticizes research that claims to have proven their troublesomeness to be covered, especially when that study has been conducted by very reputable social scientists who supported stricter gun controls before they critically analyzed the scholarly literature on the subject? Here is an obvious anomaly that cannot be readily dismissed by labeling the researchers as stooges of the National Rifle Association, so because nothing much can be reported about this study without calling into question the unquestionable, nothing much is reported about it. According to Wright, the relatively few newspaper reviewers who reviewed *Under the Gun* were impressed by the book, but this does not mean that these reviews have had any impact outside of the book review sections of the papers that carried them.

The early 1980s have produced many gun control events that have made headlines across the nation—Morton Grove, Illinois' handgun ban via village trustees' vote encouraged

11

some other city governments to follow suit and still others to follow the lead of Kennesaw, Georgia and require residents to possess firearms; the Supreme Court refused to rule on the constitutionality of the Morton Grove ban (which does not mean, as many media commentators claimed, that the Court has ruled in favor of the collective-right-to-bear-arms interpretation of the Second Amendment); San Francisco banned handguns, but the ban was overturned on the grounds that it violated California's state constitution; a handgun freeze referendum was defeated in California; and now there is a ruckus over the outlawing of Teflon-coated bullets that can penetrate the soft body armor often worn by policemen. Yet not only have the many pro-control editorials and columns commenting on these events that I have read shown no familiarity with Wright and Rossi, but many of the news reports of these events have reflected one or more of the three unquestioned assumptions.

For example, on January 11, 1984, *The Evansville Courier* carried an Associated Press news brief headed, "Gun toting town has crime increase," which began "Kennesaw, the first city in the nation to require residents to own and maintain firearms, was the only city in Cobb County with an increase in crime last year, statistics show." One armed robbery and one attempted rape (no gun involved) in 1983 increased crimes of this sort by 100% over 1982, and crime increased overall by 9% during this period, while county crime was decreasing by 5%. Thefts accounted for most of the community's crime increase. But as a well-informed reader pointed out through a letter to the editor, the AP story "failed to mention that in 1981, the year before Kennesaw passed its controversial law, there were 17 violent crimes in town: nine assaults, three rapes, four armed robberies and one homicide. In other words, violent crimes fell from 17 in 1981 to one in 1982, but then went up to three in 1983." And Kennesaw's dramatic decrease in residential burglaries from 55 in 1981 (before the law), to 19 in 1982 and nine in 1983 was ignored. A little selective perception and reporting helped to maintain the guns-are-troublesome assumption. On the other hand, three months earlier, on October 7, 1983, *The Evansville Press* carried a story by a Scripps-Howard staff reporter under the headline "Dire predictions of crime wave after handgun ban prove false." The article was about Morton Grove, of course, but what it did not mention was that the residents of that Chicago suburb had turned in only 13 handguns to the police at that time. How can the effect on crime of a handgun ban be determined if that ban has been ignored widely? An article in the October 4, 1982 issue of *Newsweek* acknowledged Kennesaw's decrease in burglaries, but reported that neither Morton Grove's handgun ban nor Kennesaw's mandatory gun ownership law appeared to have had a clearly discernible effect on crime in these communities. Then *Newsweek* took a less than subtle shot at Kennesaw—the photograph accompanying this article was of a bearded, vested, bare-chested Kennesawian packing two handguns, surely a typical citizen of this backwoods community and an example of the extremes to which the license encouraged by such an ordinance can be carried. And why had so few handguns been turned in to the Morton Grove police? "Police think residents gave most of their guns to friends and relatives living elsewhere or left them at registered gun clubs, which is perfectly legal." If the police believe most handgun owners have done this, they had better beware of Brooklyn Bridge salesmen. But back to the anomalies!

If guns are troublesome unto themselves, what is to be made of Switzerland where hunting and target shooting are very popular, and where, aside from the weapons that citizens acquire for use in these sports, the government provides practically the whole able-bodied male population between the ages of 20 and 50 (55 for officers) with military weapons for militia use? As Wright and company found, the United States is not the only modern nation with a heavily-armed civil populace, and since Switzerland has hardly any gun crime and has not been involved in a war for ages, we have another anomaly. Though comparisons between the United States and other modern nations with respect to gun crime and gun control are commonly found in the media, little is said about Switzerland. But sometimes the Swiss cannot be avoided, as syndicated columnist Sydney Harris found out recently through the letter response to a column of his in which he forthrightly took the guns-are-troublesome position. Rather than question the unquestionable, Harris indignantly tried to salvage his claims in a second column by arguing that the Swiss, though armed, keep strict control over the weapons in civilian hands, and that the government issues only rifles to militiamen. Here we have another journalistic attempt at handling gun-issue anomalies through shallow and selective examination, most likely fostered by an almost complete reliance on the pro-gun-control organizations for information on the subject. Actually, while the Swiss government keeps track of militia weapons and specifies how they can be used legally, sporting rifles and shotguns apparently are subject to no regulation and civilian handguns require only an easy-to-get permit and registration. How any of these minimal restrictions can keep guns in civilian hands from being misused (if guns are inherently troublesome) escapes me. And the Swiss do not only issue rifles to their militiamen; they issue whatever weapons are required by the individual militiaman's specialty—including full-automatic rifles and submachine guns (weapons difficult for American civilians to possess legally) as well as handguns. In other words, the anomaly does not go away, but it can be creatively avoided, as Harris has done.

And how are the major media to treat the gun-issue anomaly of anomalies? If guns, especially handguns, are troublesome unto themselves, and people who acquire such weapons for personal protection are simply asking for trouble, as *The New York Times* and other major urban newspapers and the networks regularly warn, what are the media to make of the fact that the publisher of *The New York Times*, A. O. Sulzberger, possesses a permit not only to own but to carry a handgun, a permit that ordinary New Yorkers find almost impossible to obtain? The media have made almost nothing of this matter, which suggests that more than a little elitist insincerity might be involved in the promotion of assumptions that are to be accepted unquestioningly. *The Wall Street Journal* and *New York Daily News* broke this story in 1981, but *The Times* and other newspapers crusading for gun controls have let it lie.

If all reasonable and informed Americans want strict gun controls, how are the media to handle the 4,690,734 to 2,776,973 defeat of a handgun freeze via referendum in California in 1982 and the 1,669,945 to 743,014 defeat of a handgun ban via referendum in liberal Massachusetts in 1976—the only two statewide gun control referenda conducted to date. Another anomaly, this one again handled by reporting as little as possible about these defeats. Morton Grove, Illinois' handgun ban via a 4 to 2 village trustees' vote, by way of comparison, made headlines across the country. But to the extent that comments could not be avoided, the powerful "gun lobby" was blamed for thwarting the will of the people again. The issue of *Newsweek* that came out the day before the November 2 election in California, when those polls accepted by the media were claiming that the Proposition 15 vote was too close to call (it initially enjoyed 2 to 1 support) carried a two-and-a-half column article about that proposition. The post-election issue of *Newsweek* carried a 5-line comment acknowledging the rejection of the proposition and implying that the "gun lobby" had bought victory. One of our local dailies, anticipating the defeat of the proposition, took the "gun lobby" to task a few days before the election; after the election one local paper briefly reported the propositions' rejection. Four months after Proposition 15's defeat, *The Wall Street Journal* carried a column by supporters of that proposition who claimed that valuable lessons had been learned from this first statewide confrontation with the "gun lobby" (conveniently ignoring Massachusetts in 1976), and that gun control victories were assured in the future.

According to typical media analyses of these referenda defeats, the "gun lobby" simply spent its way to victory. In California, for example, though estimates on expenditures vary, it is generally claimed that the "gun lobby" outspent supporters of Proposition 15 by a margin of three to one. But these media analysts seldom mention that while the opponents of the proposition had to purchase media time and space to promote their position, the pro-control forces had the almost unanimous free support of the California media and even some free support from the national media. As University of Illinois sociologist David Bordua has noted, the 15-minute pro-gun-control segment of "60 Minutes" that was aired nine days before the vote on Proposition 15 *alone* would have cost about $6,000,000 at that program's going rate for advertising time of about $200,000 per 30 seconds. Opponents of the proposition spent a *total* of about $6,000,000 to defeat the measure. No comment from the major media.

If all reasonable and informed Americans want strict gun controls, then it follows that only unreasonable or uninformed Americans, or those who have been misinformed by the "gun lobby," are left to oppose such measures. Therefore, the anomaly created by the decisive rejections of these referenda is dealt with typically by the major media by relegating a large portion of the eligible voters of Massachusetts (a 77% voter turnout for a better than 2 to 1 defeat) and of California (a 72% voter turnout for an almost 2 to 1 defeat) to either the unreasonable, the uninformed, or the misinformed categories—particularly the last—despite the massive free support given to these referenda by the media.

But the anomaly still persists, since critics of gun controls such as the following, all of whom have researched extensively one or more aspects of the issue, cannot easily be dismissed as being unreasonable, uninformed, or misinformed: Colin Greenwood, Cambridge University scholar and Chief Inspector of the West Yorkshire Constabulary; Joyce Lee Malcolm, Harvard Law School authority on the English Common Law origins of the Bill of Rights; John Kaplan, the Jackson Eli Reynolds Professor of Law at Stanford University; Mark K. Benenson, New York attorney and past chairman and present legal advisor of the American chapter of Amnesty International; David Bordua, prominent University of Illinois sociologist; Don B. Kates,

Jr., San Francisco civil liberties attorney and ex-civil rights activist in the South; and, of course, sociologists Wright and Rossi. Though a couple of articles that I have read have covered Kates and Benenson as liberal critics of gun controls, the major media have yet to publicize the existence of the preceding collection of extremely well-informed and impressively- credentialed gun control critics or to publicize the existence of the collection of devastating scholarly critiques of such measures that these individuals and others have produced. It will be interesting to see what the media do with Kates' recently released book, *Firearms and Violence: Issues of Public Policy*, which contains articles by a number of scholarly critics of gun controls. Kates' earlier book, *Restricting Handguns: The Liberal Skeptics Speak Out*, foreworded by the late liberal senator Frank Church, received favorable reviews from *The New York Times, The Los Angeles Times,* and other publications supportive of gun controls, but like Wright and Rossi's work, it seems not to have caused many establishment editors, columnists, and reporters to question the three sacred assumptions.

Neither have the media at the national level seemed interested in publicizing the fact that 55 of 58 California sheriffs, over 100 police chiefs, and 33 law enforcement organizations opposed Proposition 15. And the media have seemed puzzled by the fact that both the U.S. Treasury and the U.S. Justice Departments oppose recently-proposed legislation aimed at outlawing the armor-piercing "cop killer" bullet that apparently has yet to kill or wound a cop. So puzzled, in fact, are the media, that much editorializing has taken the NRA to task for opposing this legislation without mentioning the opposition of these departments. The anomaly created by the opposition to various gun controls

18

by apparently reasonable, well-informed people remains, as does the media's means of coping with anomalies.

If other modern, urban, industrial nations (England and Japan are those generally mentioned) have solved their "gun problems" through gun controls, then what are the media to make of *Firearms Control: A Study of Armed Crime and Firearms Control in England and Wales,* by the aforementioned Chief Inspector Greenwood, the only thorough study of the effectiveness of gun controls in England and Wales done to date? Strict English gun controls were not enacted until 1920, and according to Greenwood, "No matter how one approaches the figures, one is forced to the rather startling conclusion that the use of firearms in crime was very much less when there were no controls of any sort and when anyone, convicted criminal or lunatic, could buy any type of firearm without restriction." Though Greenwood's book was published back in 1972 by the respected publishing house of Routledge & Kegan Paul of London, and though it has received quite a bit of publicity in the gun press in this country, if the major media have ever so much as acknowledged the existence of this work, I am not aware of it. And I have yet to run across a major media commentary on gun crime or gun control in Japan that shows awareness of the fact that for various historical, political, cultural, and geographic reasons, the civilian possession of guns has never been widespread in that country. Cross-cultural comparisons of crime rates, always a risky business, abound in the media, of course, but seldom if ever is it pointed out that the murder rate among Japanese-Americans, who have easy access to firearms, is lower than the murder rate in Japan where firearms possession has never been widespread, or that the Japanese suicide rate is twice as high as the American rate, in spite of the fact that Americans have easy access to guns and the Japanese do not. Nor do the media have much to say about such countries as France, where, according to French firearms authority Michel Josserand, strict gun controls are widely ignored.

Therefore, despite the fact that critics of gun controls as well as more or less balanced analysts of such measures have been able to penetrate the major and lesser media increasingly in recent years, and despite the existence of countless anomalies of the sort that have been mentioned, the assumptions that guns themselves (especially handguns) are troublesome, that Americans want laws that would strictly regulate or even prohibit the civilian possession of guns (especially handguns), and that other modern nations have effectively regulated guns and reduced gun crime through such measures continue to permeate heavily major media coverage of the gun issue in the United States. What is the explanation for the persistence of these assumptions? To begin with, to anyone who knows much about guns and the wide range of legitimate uses to which they are put, it is quite obvious that many media folk who report or comment on the gun issue know very little about guns and almost nothing about the wide range of legitimate uses to which guns, including handguns, are put. Neither do these individuals have more than superficial knowledge concerning the criminal use of guns. Anomalies may often be ignored, therefore, because reporters and commentators are honestly unaware of their existence and the assumptions that they accept do not encourage questioning. But there are apparently a significant number of major media folks in positions that allow them to express their own views through the media or to decide what views will be expressed who have vested interests in ignoring anomalies and by hook or by crook keeping these assumptions unquestioned by others, or possibly even by themselves.

Gun Week editor Joseph P. Tartaro has compared the media's reaction to the scholarly gun studies done by Wright, Rossi, and others with the Roman Catholic church's reaction to Galileo's work. "Given the opportunity many journalists of print and electronic genre would still like to see science and scholars who disprove their superstitions burned at the stake. In many cases, they have excommunicated such thoughts and thinkers from the news church by exorcising them from their pages and broadcasts." I fully agree with Tartaro, and I suspect that those individuals to whom he refers can be divided, though not neatly, into two groups, both of which are for all practical purposes part of the gun control movement. One group is composed of sincere reformers to whom the three assumptions about guns are articles of faith, part and parcel of the urban, upper-middle class (or aspiring upper-middle class), liberal world view that seems to permeate media circles as well as intellectual circles in general. These individuals believe that the world would be a better place without guns, and as is commonly the case with "true believers" and prohibitionists, they do not care to have their views challenged. The other group is composed of elitists (such as Sulzberger) who themselves have nothing against guns, but who want to keep guns out of the hands not only of criminals but of the potentially troublesome common man. The evidence suggests that neither media reformers nor media elitists balk at creative or at least selective reporting or commentating on the gun issue. At any rate, whether the general scandalously unprofessional media coverage of the gun issue is primarily the product of honest media ignorance, media reformist zeal, media elitist tendencies, or some combination of all of these, the end result comes much too close to an Orwellian 1984-ish scenario for comfort.

BIG JOURNALISM'S WAR ON THE SECOND AMENDMENT

Original manuscript of an essay first published as "Shooting Blind" in Reason, November, 1995, and reprinted in Gun News Digest, *Spring, 1996.*

In a September, 1988 "report on assault weapons" that he prepared for the Education Fund to end Handgun Violence and New Right Watch, Josh Sugarmann candidly stated: "The weapons' menacing looks, coupled with the public's confusion over fully automatic machine guns versus semi-automatic assault weapons—anything that looks like a machine gun is assumed to be a machine gun—can only increase the chance of public support for restrictions on these weapons. In addition, few people can envision a practical use for these guns."

So back in 1988, one of the nation's leading gun prohibitionists was banking on public support for restrictions on "semi-automatic assault weapons," not because that public was informed about the guns so labeled but because it was uninformed about them and likely to remain so. And Sugarmann knew what he was talking about. Large segments of that public still do not know the difference between machine guns and semiautomatics, and cannot envision a practical use for high-tech-looking semiautomatics. So what are we to make of the polls that invariably indicate about 70 percent public support for an "assault weapon" ban? These were the polls, after all, that apparently persuaded many uninformed and/or public-opinion-conscious politicians to vote for the crime bill with its "assault weapon" ban.

And how could Sugarmann be so sure that the public would remain uninformed enough about "assault weapons" to support a ban on guns so labeled? We are supposed to have a free press, after all, and that free press, we are continually told by journalists, acts as our public watchdog by keeping us informed about all sides of controversial issues. However, as an astute observer of such things, Sugarmann must have known that, for the most part, big journalism (the major TV networks, major newspapers and news and general-interest magazines) has long inadvertently or purposely been in league with the gun-prohibitionist movement. The ways that big journalism helped Sugarmann and friends confuse the public about "assault weapons" are worth examining, because the "assault weapon" ban was being challenged by segments of the new Congress before the bombing of the federal building in Oklahoma City, and big journalism was showing no willingness to clear up the confusion it helped create. And since that mindless bombing, Congress has put the ban challenge on hold as big journalism has uncritically joined the attack on the militia movement and the National Rifle Association.

Big Journalism and Guns: Ignorance and/or Chicanery

Machine guns are *automatics*—they fire as long as the trigger is held back—and the legal possession of such guns by American citizens has been strictly regulated by the federal government since 1934; they have long been banned in some states; and no new automatics have been allowed to enter civilian circulation legally since 1986. Though the constitutionality of these restrictions on machine gun ownership is questionable, given the political climate on guns, any such questioning is not likely to get very far.

Semiautomatics, on the other hand, regardless of how much some of them may look like machine guns, fire one shot per trigger pull, and they have been in common civilian use for recreation and self-defense since the turn of the century. Since the guns called "assault rifles" by the military fire either automatic or *burst fire* (a few shots per trigger pull) as well as semiautomatic, a gun that fires semiautomatic only is not an "assault" anything regardless of how it looks or what people like Sugarmann claim. So why the confusion?

The confusion may exist partly because of innocent common usage. Until the "assault weapon" hysteria, not only gun users but gun manufacturers commonly referred to ordinary civilian semiautomatic shotguns, rifles, and pistols as automatic shotguns, etc. This practice has never confused knowledgeable gun people, but it may have confused uninformed journalists and played into the hands of gun prohibitionists like Sugarmann who thrive on confusion. However, ignorance alone cannot explain big journalism's Orwellian treatment of the "assault weapon" issue over the past decade.

Newsweek helped launch the "assault weapon" hysteria three years before Sugarmann's "report" with its October 14, 1985 cover story, "Machine Gun USA." While this article acknowledged the difference between semiautomatics and automatics, it implied that the former could be converted to the latter so easily that the difference made no difference, and it carried illustrations of several semiautomatic variations of automatic weapons *accompanied by the much higher firing rates of the latter.* However, big journalism's misinformation and disinformation campaign against "assault weapons" did not hit its stride until after the January 17, 1989 Stockton, California schoolyard shooting perpetrated by an emotionally disturbed individual armed with a semiautomatic version of the Soviet AK-47 assault rifle. Print journalism's news and commentary coverage of this and subsequent "assault weapon" developments regularly confused semiautomatics with automatics/machine guns, but if one picture is actually worth a thousand words, the Orwell *1984* Award for confusing the public on this issue goes to TV's NBC with a second to CNN.

Since the Stockton shootings back in 1989, these two networks have often shown their viewers demonstrations of machine guns spewing out bullets at an impressive rate while one-shot-per-trigger-pull semiautomatics were being discussed. Viewers who knew no better were thereby led to believe that semiautomatics are machine guns. Several times over this period, NBC carried this deception a step further. While a machine gun was being demonstrated, a gun-control advocate explained to his/her interviewer and the TV audience that the semiautomatics to be regulated by the legislation being discussed have no hunting or other sporting uses. The impression was not only thereby given that the gun being demonstrated was the type of gun to be banned (which it was not), but that opponents of the ban want to hunt with machine guns (which they do not), and that sport is the only legitimate use for which Americans need guns (which it is not).

I have shown these juxtapositions of machine gun demonstrations with semiautomatic commentaries to introductory sociology classes. Out of over 250 students who have viewed these juxtapositions, which last only a matter of seconds, a dozen and a half indicated that they recognized that the machine gun being demonstrated was not a semiautomatic. So how much of that 70% public support for a ban on "assault weapons" was actually support for a ban on already heavily-restricted machine guns? And what do we have here, an Orwellian jewel or evidence of honest journalistic ignorance? Honest ignorance and a rush to meet deadlines, says David McCormick, NBC's man in charge of broadcast standards. I spoke to him by phone on August 16, 1994, the day after I called to complain about NBC's latest juxtaposition. The gentleman who answered that call excused the juxtaposition as a mistake, and hung up on me when I pointed out that NBC had been making that same mistake for five years. When I called back to get his name, he told me that he did not have to take abuse and hung up again. Mr. McCormick was quite pleasant, however, even after I informed him that ignorance seems a lame excuse for the misleading juxtapositions that *NBC* has aired for five years. After all, heads rolled at NBC over their single assisted explosion of a GM truck, but the network has yet to even acknowledge misleading the public for years concerning "assault weapons." I have since found out that NBC even aired one of these juxtapositions shortly after Wayne LaPierre of the National Rifle Association spent several hours demonstrating the difference between semiautomatics and machine guns to an NBC crew.

Unlike NBC and CNN, CBS early acknowledged the difference between machine guns and semiautomatics through its March 16, 1989 special live edition of *48 Hours* dealing with the alleged threat to the public posed by "assault weapons." Like *Newsweek's* 1985 offering, however, CBS made light of that difference. Semiautomatics can be fired fast enough and with better control than machine guns can be fired, noted reporter David Martin as he fired a true assault rifle in the semiautomatic mode after firing it full automatic. He did not demonstrate (or even mention) more conventional-looking semiautomatic sporting guns that can be fired just as fast as the high-tech-looking semiautomatics and have been in common civilian use since the turn of the century. Martin also made much over the firepower of guns equipped with large capacity magazines. He did not mention that magazines can be changed so quickly that three 10-round magazines can produce nearly the same firepower as one 30-round magazine. Of course, ignorance rather than chicanery may account for Martin's incomplete reportage on these issues, but it cannot explain all of his treatment of these guns.

In 1889, gun designing genius John Browning converted a lever-action rifle to a machine gun. During World War II, the Australians converted many bolt-action rifles to machine guns. For decades the Pathans of Hindu-Kush have produced automatic weapons from scratch in shops far less sophisticated than those that can be found in countless basements and garages across the United States. Any competent machinist who knows guns can do these things, but it is the claim of the gun prohibitionists that "semiautomatic assault weapons" can *easily* and *quickly* be converted to machine guns. Never mind that it is illegal to carry out such a conversion, or that ease of conversion to a restricted configuration can justify banning all rifles and shotguns on the grounds that they are all easily hacksaw-convertible to sawed-off weapons. Ignorance on reporter Martin's part again? Probably. However, he went beyond ignorance to try to prove that "semiautomatic assault weapons" are simply waiting for illegal conversion, and claimed to have spent less than two hours finding a gunsmith willing to do such a job—a job that took only nine minutes.

Viewers saw only about 15 seconds of the alleged conversion, not enough for even the Bureau of Alcohol, Tobacco and Firearms to determine if it had actually been carried out, though BATF did reprimand CBS by letter. In a letter to a complaining viewer, CBS claimed that the conversion had been completed, but that the gun had then been immediately converted back to semiautomatic. If the gun was not fired, how did Martin know that it was in fact converted to a machine gun? Since reporter Martin was shown firing an *automatic* rifle immediately after the brief conversion footage, however, viewers were led to believe that they were seeing the results of that conversion—unless they knew enough to recognize that the gun being worked on was not an Ml6 variant like the type being fired. *So we only have CBS's claim that a workable conversion was carried out at all, let alone in 9 minutes. If it was carried out, CBS violated federal law and received no more than a letter reprimand for doing so. If it was not carried out, CBS lied to its viewers.* Either way, CBS went out of its way to contribute to the demonization of "semiautomatic assault weapons" and to further the cause of the gun prohibitionists.

In a later segment of this same *48 Hours* special, reporter Bernard Goldberg interviewed a Florida gun manufacturer. As Goldberg prattled on about the company's guns being used by drug dealers and other criminals, viewers got glimpses of menacing-looking pistols being test fired and prepared for shipment. Uninformed viewers probably did not recognize that the "assault pistols" shown, despite their menacing looks, were chambered for the low-powered .22 cartridge that has been a recreational favorite since the late 19th century. No mention was made of this fact. Big journalism's coverage of "assault weapons" has seldom mentioned that the guns so labeled are chambered for cartridges commonly used for recreation and/or self defense. In fact, this coverage has more often than not claimed that these guns are extraordinarily powerful, and on occasion journalists have even resorted to fakery to support this false claim.

Since the 1989 Stockton schoolyard shooting, films of watermelons being splattered by bullets have been used on occasion by both print and electronic journalists to illustrate the alleged extraordinary power of the AK-47-type rifle used in that shooting. Shortly after Stockton, a reporter and photographer from the now-defunct *Los Angeles Herald Examiner* asked a Los Angeles County deputy sheriff to demonstrate AK-47 power by shooting a watermelon with one. The deputy replied that firing the full-metal-jacketed, military ammunition used at Stockton the gun would simply put a hole in the melon, and that is exactly what happened when he shot it. The reporter then asked the deputy to shoot a melon with his pistol, and he did so. Though far less powerful than the rifle, his 9mm pistol fired an expanding hollow-point slug that splattered its melon impressively. Both the puncturing of a melon by the *more* powerful rifle and the splattering of a melon by the *less* powerful pistol were captured on film. The *Herald Examiner* then published the photograph of the melon being splattered by the deputy's pistol—but *credited the splattering to the* rifle.

About that time, splattered-watermelon demonstrations started appearing on KABC Los Angeles and other California stations as well as nationally, but their connection to the *Herald Examiner* fakery, if any, is not clear. It is at least possible that some of these TV splatterings were honest, since as gun control opponent Neal Knox found, military-style 7.62x39mm slugs fired from an AK-47 can splatter a watermelon, apparently depending on the latter's ripeness and other variables. Even if these TV splatterings were actually produced by AK-47s, however, they were still deceptive unless they also showed what ordinary guns will do to a melon, as an ABC Peter Jennings special did on January 24, 1990. While this honest ABC demonstration showed an AK-47 putting baseball-sized holes in watermelons, and the Neal Knox demonstration filmed for Gun Owners of America showed one *splattering* a melon, both of these demonstrations also showed common sporting guns *vaporizing* watermelons.

The "assault *rifle*" concept is of World War II German origin, and came to be accepted by the major postwar powers. Such rifles combine the spray-fire capabilities of the *less* powerful submachine guns and the one-shot-per-trigger-pull, aimed-fire capabilities of the *more* powerful battle rifles of this century's wars. Assault rifles are less powerful than traditional military rifles, *which are chambered for cartridges long used for hunting and target shooting* (1) because cartridge sizes have been reduced so that more of them can be carried in magazines and on individual soldiers to feed guns capable of firing 10 or more rounds per second, and (2) because it was necessary to reduce recoil to make such guns controllable during automatic fire. Since legal machine gun ownership by civilians is strictly regulated in the United States, *semiautomatic-only* variations of assault rifles, submachine guns, and other *automatic* firearms have been offered by both domestic and foreign makers for civilian sale in this country. Though the label is quite elastic, it is for the most part these high-tech-looking guns that are now called "semiautomatic assault weapons" by Sugarmann and his gun-prohibitionist friends. Of course, the misleading

31

"assault weapon" label is of great value to their cause because it sounds like something for which civilians *should* have no use. However, such guns have a number of legitimate civilian uses easily discoverable by any journalist curious enough to look for them. Few have looked.

Though American shooters were not immediately attracted by the non-traditional appearance of these otherwise generally non-remarkable guns, their durability and, ironically, even their media-generated notoriety have helped to increase interest in them. Since for the first time in our history American troops are equipped with rifles of a type (automatic or burst fire) difficult or (in some states) impossible for civilians to own legally, civilians interested in the military-style rifle matches *long supported by the federal government* must use semiautomatic-only variations of our recent and current military rifles. Many farmers and ranchers in sparsely settled areas have accepted certain models of these light but durable military-style semiautomatics as varmint and utility rifles. Boaters off the drug-runner-infested coast of Florida also seem to have acquired an interest in such guns, but on the lighter side, so have collectors and hobbyists. In other words, it is utter and easily provable nonsense to claim that civilians have no practical, sporting, or recreational uses for these military-style semiautomatics. But the primary use American civilians have for these guns has nothing to do with recreation or even with defense against criminals.

What Second Amendment?

The Second Amendment to the United States Constitution states: "A well regulated militia being necessary to the security of a free State, the right of the people to keep and bear Arms, shall not be infringed." This amendment is seldom even mentioned in establishment news coverage of the gun issue, even though opposition to gun controls is primarily rooted in it. With the exceptions of 1983 public TV and 1993 A&E documentaries, a May 22, 1995 *U.S. News & World Report* article, and a few conservative, libertarian, or populist columnists, what little journalistic commentary does mention the amendment almost invariably claims that its meaning is unclear, that it is outdated and should be repealed, or that it only protects the right of the National Guard to possess guns.

However, the meaning of the Second Amendment is very clear to the vast majority of scholars who have *actually examined* the paper trail on it left by the Founders. Perhaps James Madison's friend Tench Coxe expressed their concerns most succinctly: "As civil rulers, not having their duty to the people duly before them, may attempt to tyrannize, and as the military forces which must be occasionally raised to defend our country, might pervert their power to the injury of their fellow citizens, the people are confirmed by the next article in their right to keep and bear their *private* arms" (emphasis added).

The Founders also made it clear that the whole armed people were the militia. The Federalist Papers and other writings indicate that they feared large professional military forces and National Guard-type select militia—both of which we now have. Citizens and their privately-owned guns were just another part of the system of checks and balances that the Founders felt was necessary to keep any government from drifting into tyranny. This fear of theirs permeates their writings and the Bill of Rights itself, but no longer concerns most journalists *unless the First Amendment is threatened.* It is also important to note that the Bill of Rights was not seen by its supporters as granting rights. It was a written guarantee that government would not deny certain already existing "natural rights" to its citizens. Authors of the 50 law-review articles that support this interpretation include such prominent, liberal, non-gun-owning scholars as Sanford Levinson of the University of Texas, Akhil R. Amar of Yale, and William Van Alstyne of Duke.

According to *Title 10, U. S. CODE , Section 311*, the National Guard is still only the organized part of a militia that consists of practically all able-bodied males and some females between 17 and 45 years of age who are citizens of the United States or have declared an intention to become citizens. The only 20th-century United States Supreme Court ruling (United States v. Miller, 1939) touching on the Second Amendment acknowledged that militiamen called to service "were expected to *appear bearing arms supplied by themselves and of the kind in common use at the time*" (emphasis added). In 1939, American troops were equipped with semiautomatic pistols and were being equipped with semiautomatic rifles. Now our troops are equipped with less powerful but higher-magazine-capacity semiautomatic pistols and less powerful but burst-fire and higher-magazine-capacity rifles.

American citizens have traditionally had access to rifles and pistols with more power and firepower than those issued to common soldiers, and in keeping with the traditional American views on the militia, the Army's Office of the Director of Civilian Marksmanship has long sold surplus pistols, rifles, and carbines, including semiautomatics, to the public at bargain-basement prices. There have been no claims that Americans have caused problems with these surplus military small arms. Yet since common soldiers have been issued automatic or burst-fire rifles, American citizens no longer have access to up-to-date military small arms, and the "assault weapon" ban now even restricts their access to semiautomatic variations of these guns. *So now we not only have the large professional military and select militia that the Founders feared, but there is a movement afoot to get militarily-effective small arms out of civilian hands. There has been no big-journalistic examination of the people-control and constitutional implications of these efforts.* In fact, and ironically, big journalists regularly uncritically present big city police chiefs, the heads of armed *government* agencies, as detached experts supporting gun restrictions in the public interest.

Instead of regularly and uncritically aiding gun prohibitionist efforts to demonize "semiautomatic assault weapons," even to the extent of using misleading demonstrations of the kind I have described, what if big journalism had regularly and accurately informed the public about these guns? Instead of ignoring or deriding the Second Amendment, what if big journalism had regularly informed the public about the purpose of that amendment as clearly stated in the paper trail left by the Founders and discovered by those current scholars with enough integrity to examine that paper trail before commenting on the amendment's meaning? If big journalism had regularly done these things, I seriously doubt that pollsters would find anything close to 70 percent public support for restrictions on the possession of "assault weapons." *Politicians might also better understand that the rights guaranteed by the Bill of Rights are not dependent on the support of public opinion for their continued existence, and cannot be repealed by a government that did not grant them.*

Even Mike Moore, the editor of *The Quill* , the magazine of the Society of Professional Journalists, who does not own a gun and who apparently believes that there are more "really strange people" in the NRA than there are in his journalist's society, acknowledged in a March, 1990 column titled "The Second Amendment gets no respect," that "in 30 years in the business it's hard to imagine a subject—guns, and their use, their misuse, and their control—that has inspired more poor reporting and silly editorial commentary." Much of that poor reporting and silly commentary surely is ignorance based. Ted Gest of *U.S. News & World Report* acknowledged in a 1992 *Media Studies Journal* article on journalistic inadequacies in gun-issue coverage that few of today's journalists know much about guns. In an article introducing *USA Today's* extended examination of the gun issue at the end of 1993, Tony Mauro wrote that in his newspaper's newsroom, "which prides itself on drawing its staff from a cross section of the nation, it was hard to find editors and reporters who had ever pulled a trigger." If ignorance explains sloppy reporting and commentary on the gun issue that has been going on for decades, however, journalists apparently are not interested in overcoming that ignorance by learning about guns and the legitimate uses to which they are regularly put by millions of Americans. Also, since journalistic misinformation and disinformation on guns invariably favor the gun prohibitionists, something more than ignorance must be involved.

The Politics of Premise Pushing

Major syndicated columnists and editors of major newspapers who have not taken a strong stand in print in support of the most restrictive gun controls are few in number. Michael Gartner, before he was sacked as president of NBC News over the GM-truck scam, even used a guest column in *USA Today* to call for the repeal of the Second Amendment. However, journalists have long maintained that they keep their personal views firmly in check when they engage in reporting as opposed to commentary. "Give light and the people will find their own way," and all that we-just-tell-it-like-it-is-and-let-the-chips-fall-where-they-may business. Some rather prominent journalists are no longer even trying to maintain that fiction when covering the gun issue. When guns are concerned, it seems that only premise-supporting evidence is sought out. And big journalism's working premise is that the battle over guns and their control is between the American public, its police protectors, and its responsible representatives, aided by neutral researchers and the watchdog press, on one side, against the "gun lobby," headed by the NRA and representing no more than the gun industry and other irresponsible vested interests, on the other.

Bill Peters, news correspondent for Los Angeles' ABC-owned stations, could thereby tell the U.S. Senate in 1989 that "today it is our [journalism's] responsibility—using all the powerful means we have at our disposal . . . both to inform the public of the danger to society posed by military assault rifles and to help build support for getting rid of them." Forget the Second Amendment, and never mind that official studies conducted in California and other states such as Florida and New Jersey, and cities such as Los Angeles, San Francisco, Chicago, Miami, New York, and Washington, D.C., have found that these rather ordinary guns are seldom criminally misused. Though some of these studies were conducted in hotbeds of violent crime, not one of them indicated that more than 3.7% of the guns used in homicides or 3.9% of the guns seized by the police, whether or not they had been criminally misused, are "assault weapons."

Gloria Hammond, of *Time's* editorial office, informed readers who complained of bias in that magazine's July 17, 1989 gun-issue cover story that "the time for opinions on the dangers of gun availability is long since gone, replaced by overwhelming evidence that it represents a growing threat to public safety." *Time* has shown no sign of changing its position, even though the most sophisticated studies conducted before and after 1989 by such prominent social scientists as James D. Wright, Peter H. Rossi (a former president of the American Sociological Association), and Gary Kleck (a winner of the American Society of Criminology's prestigious Hindelang Award), have demolished the guns-are-troublesome hypothesis. *Time's* news hounds also ignored the fact that gun-ownership rates in this country are far higher in small-town and rural areas than they are in large urban areas, yet the latter areas generally have far higher violent-crime rates than the former. Also, the Swiss have only 1.8 homicides per 100,000 (compared to around 10 for us) in spite of the fact that practically every male between the ages of 20 and 50 keeps a *government-issued full-automatic assault rifle* and ammunition for it in his home. And the Israeli homicide rate is also 1.8, even though Israelis have easy access to military small arms through *government loans* and have *government* encouragement to carry handguns.

Thomas Winship, a former editor of the *Boston Globe* who now chairs the Center for Foreign Journalists in Reston, Virginia, called for a newspaper crusade against guns in his April 24, 1993 *Editor & Publisher* column. He urged editors he assumed to be as anti-gun as himself to "Investigate the NRA with renewed vigor. . . . Print names of elected officials who take NRA funds. Support all forms of gun licensing; in fact all the causes NRA opposes." So much for let-the-chips-fall-where-they-may journalism. Winship sees no need to investigate the myth-makers who have given us (1) "Saturday night special" handguns imprecisely defined as "small" and "cheap," that miraculously are devastating in the hands of criminals but useless for defense against criminals; (2) Teflon-coated "cop killer bullets" that were developed for the police, were not available to the public, and were around for 13 years without penetrating body armor to kill a cop before NBC in 1982 breathlessly informed the public of the hazards they posed for the police; (3) metal-detector-defeating "plastic pistols," terrorist guns to the intrepid investigative reporter Jack Anderson, that actually contain about a pound of steel and are now standard issue for the Austrian Army and many American cops; and (4) "semiautomatic assault weapons." Had it not been for the rare big-journalistic integrity exhibited by ABC's *Nightline*, Winshipian journalists at *Newsweek* and elsewhere may well have revived the "cop-killer bullet" myth through the Rhino/ Black Rhino flap of late 1994.

So back in 1988, Josh Sugarmann accurately read big journalism. He and his friends did not have to worry about the let-the-chips-fall-where-they-may reporting that would put their gun-prohibitionist movement out of business. It almost seems that big journalism has become, for the most part, little more than a purveyor of the enlightened conventional wisdom on controversial issues like gun control. And that enlightened conventional wisdom seems to have been defined by upper-middle-class, urban-oriented, cosmopolitan segments of American society that wish to make over American society as a whole to their satisfaction and fear resistance from an armed citizenry. Social engineers are leery of the Bill of Rights in general and of the Second Amendment in particular, so Orwellian big journalistic attempts to denigrate, ignore, or redefine that amendment will surely continue. However, since talk radio, cable TV, and computer networks are now giving informed segments of the public the opportunity to circumvent big journalism and reach the public at large, big journalism's treatment of guns and the Second Amendment is being challenged. It remains to be seen how persistent and successful this challenge will be.

THE MOST DANGEROUS AMENDMENT

Originally published in Chronicles, December, 1999, and reprinted in Gun News Digest, *Summer, 2001.*

One evening a few years back, I was channel surfing when I ran across a panel discussion of efforts to restrict children's access to smut and violence on TV. One of the panelists was former New York mayor Ed Koch; another was the president of one of the major TV networks. The latter was quite agitated by proposed regulatory measures that he felt undermined the First Amendment and paved the way to censorship. I anticipated his position; however, I didn't anticipate Koch's reply. The former mayor pointed out that the slippery-slope argument that the TV honcho was making was exactly the same as that made by those who saw all attempts at gun control as undermining the Second Amendment and paving the way to gun confiscation. Hoisted by his own petard, the TV honcho's response was hilarious. He blanched and managed to sputter out something to the effect that some slippery slopes were more desirable than others.

I can't remember who that TV executive was or what network he headed, but it really doesn't make any difference. I'd be willing to bet, and I'm not a betting man, that the vast majority of gatekeepers of the mainstream electronic and print media, entertainment as well as news, would have responded to a perceived threat to the First Amendment just as he did, and that they would have been equally nonplussed when called upon to reconcile their views on the First Amendment with their views on the Second Amendment. In

First Amendment-loving journalistic circles, "The Second Amendment gets no respect," as Mike Moore, then editor of *The Quill,* the magazine of the Society of Professional Journalists, acknowledged in a column by that title in the March, 1990 issue of his magazine. Charlton Heston, the movie actor who has become the president of the National Rifle Association, once drove home the same point before the National Press Club, and what he and Moore had to say applies to mainstream media circles in general.

In a *USA Today* column written when he was president of NBC, Michael Gartner called for the repeal of the Second Amendment. Tom Brokaw, Sam Donaldson, Michael Kinsley, George Will, Hodding Carter, Martin Schram, Leonard Larsen, Don Shoemaker, Bob Moos, Robert Reno, and the editors of the *Washington* Post have either dismissed the right to keep and bear arms as a collective right, or called it an outdated individual right that has withered away or that should be repealed. And Robert Altman, the producer of ABC's *Gun,* a blatantly anti-gun-ownership series from 1997, acknowledges that he "disdains the prevalence of guns in American homes." As he told a *Washington Post* reporter: "I don't care what the founding fathers said—they didn't have a police force to call on." In a 1993 *Editor & Publisher* column, former *Boston Globe* editor Thomas Winship ignored the Second Amendment altogether when he called for a national newspaper crusade against guns.

Parade posed the following rhetorical question, complete with answer, to anyone thinking about entering its photography contest celebrating the 1991 bicentennial of the Bill of Rights: "How would you convey the sense of the Second Amendment in a photograph? Perhaps a soldier or a Marine or a sailor or an airman departing for duty, a scene with a military flavor, a *graduation,* or maybe a National Guardsman helping in a setting unrelated to arms or battle" (emphasis added). This after informing readers that we have long since overcome the fears of the federal government that had "inspired the language of the amendment."

Life's bicentennial treatment of the Second Amendment acknowledged that an armed populace was necessary when the Bill of Rights was ratified, but made it clear that widespread gun ownership is troublesome now and that the amendment is anachronistic. A 1984 *Atlanta Constitution* political cartoon had Benjamin Franklin (who had nothing to do with the Second Amendment) commenting to his colleagues: "We'd better say it's for a 'well-regulated militia' or every nut in the country will think he has a right to own a gun." And a television special on the Bill of Rights back in the 1970s included a symbolic representation of each of the first ten amendments to the Constitution. The logo for the Second Amendment, which was given short shrift in the discussion, looked like it had been lifted off of a box of Arm and Hammer baking soda—a hammer, not a sword or a gun, gripped in a hand at the end of a muscular arm with a rolled-up sleeve. One could get the impression that the Second Amendment guaranteed us the right to *bare* our arms.

I could go on and on, but publisher Lyle Stuart's comments bring me back to my central point. Stuart once justified publishing *The Turner Diaries,* the militantly racist and anti-Semitic novel that allegedly served as convicted Oklahoma City bomber Timothy McVeigh's inspiration, in this way: "I'm a nut on just a few things in life. I've always tested the limits of the First Amendment. I'm a great believer in letting anybody publish the most outrageous, unpopular things there are." Ah, but Stuart has a social conscience.

He donates one dollar of every sale of this $12 paperback to "an anti-handgun organization." Another deep-thinking First Amendment supporter who completely ignores Second Amendment concerns.

The Founding Fathers left us a mile-wide paper trail explaining the purpose of the Second Amendment. Several scholarly books and over 60 law review articles (many of them by prominent, non-gun-owning, liberal scholars like Sanford Levinson of the University of Texas, William Van Alstyne of Duke, and Akhil Amar of Yale) have detailed this paper trail for anyone willing to take the time to read them. Consider what James Madison's friend Tench Coxe had to say on the subject before the ratification of the Bill of Rights: "As civil rulers, not having their duty to the people duly before them, may attempt to tyrannize, and as the military forces which must be occasionally raised to defend our country, might pervert their power to the injury of their fellow citizens, the people are confirmed by the next article in their right to keep and bear their *private* arms" [emphasis added].

In other words, in spite of what the *Atlanta Constitution's* cartoonist may think, the Founders did believe that every law-abiding American citizen had a right to own a gun. And the main reason that individual gun ownership was considered to be important was to keep in line the armed agents of the state that Robert Altman and the Pollyannas at *Parade* trust so much. And for the information of Tom Brokaw, Hodding Carter, and the others who believe that the Second Amendment is anachronistic and defended only by right-wing nuts in the 20th century, consider the following comment: "The right of citizens to bear arms is just one more guarantee against arbitrary government, one more safeguard against a tyranny which now appears remote in America, but which historically has proved to be always possible." The words are those of Mr. Liberal himself, the late Hubert H. Humphrey, and were circulated in a 1959 written statement on the Second Amendment, but they express sentiments that went unquestioned until the middle of this century. For the further information of people like George Will, who should know better, and Michael Gartner, who call for the repeal of the Second Amendment, the Bill of Rights guarantees rights that the Founders assumed to be natural; consequently, a government that didn't grant them can't repeal them.

Incidentally, a government that monopolizes weaponry can, among many other things, tell pundits to take their precious First Amendment and the rights it guarantees and stuff them where the sun doesn't shine. But I never cease to be amazed that so many people who believe in the power of words can, when it suits their purposes, turn a blind eye to the consequences of words and the ideas they convey.

I'm a strong supporter of all of the Bill of Rights, First Amendment, Second Amendment, and all the rest. But with those rights come responsibilities. Media elitists like Lyle Stuart want to take away the vital right to keep and bear arms (the teeth of the Bill of Rights) not only from those Americans who abuse that right by harming innocents with their guns, but from the vast majority of Americans who don't abuse it. But when it comes to the First Amendment, Stuart and company aren't even willing to acknowledge that the rights to free speech and a free press can be abused, let alone consider what should be done about those who abuse them.

Of course, abuse of the right to arms often produces a body count, while the impact of the abuse of the right to free speech and/or a free press isn't that clear cut. So Stuart can deplore the killing of innocent blacks and Jews by gun or any other means at the same time that he feels free, or even obligated, to publish books that claim that killing blacks and Jews is warranted. Men like him can decry violence as they market gangsta rap celebrating the casual killing of cops, the abuse of women, and antisocial behavior in general. They can rant and rave about the easy availability of guns being responsible for school shootings while focusing national attention on the young monsters who carry out these shootings. And they can even produce violent videogames, such as Postal, that can serve as training programs for these monsters.

I'm not suggesting government censorship. I am suggesting that Stuart and the TV executive who responded to Ed Koch should take a good long look in the mirror and assume some of the responsibility for the amoral mess that they have helped to create, instead of blaming it on inanimate objects that they in many ways have encouraged some people to misuse. And I am suggesting that far more social damage can occur through widespread media abuse of the rights guaranteed by the First Amendment than through individual abuse of the rights guaranteed by the Second Amendment. For the widespread media abuse of First Amendment rights does much to promote the normlessness and alienation responsible for, among many other unpleasant things, murders committed with guns. Less testing of the limits of the First Amendment might do more to bring about a safer society than would a repeal of the Second Amendment.

PART II

GUNS AND POPULAR CULTURE

HOLLYWOOD AND THE MEANING OF GUNS

Originally published in short form as "Guns and the Movies" in Liberty, October, 2000, and reprinted in this original form as "The Meaning of Guns in the Popular Culture" in Gun News Digest, *Winter, 2000-2001.*

It read like a Who's Who of the entertainment industry: Meryl Streep; Rosie O'Donnell; Madonna; Henry Winkler; Rosemary Clooney; Jerry Seinfeld; Barbra Streisand; Fannie Flagg; Tony Bennett; Richard Gere; Spike Lee; Jack Nicholson; Cher; Mary Tyler Moore; Dick Van Dyke; Barry Manilow; Bruce Springsteen; Moon Zappa; Richard Dreyfus; Alec Baldwin, and some 200 others. But the names of all these celebrities appeared in a Handgun Control Inc. full-page "Open Letter to the National Rifle Association" in the June 9, 1999 edition of *USA Today.*

The purpose of this letter, published in the wake of the horrendous school shootings in Littleton, Colorado, was to promote various additional gun controls—everything from the mandatory sale of trigger locks with every gun purchased to a complete ban on large-capacity magazines and "assault weapons." No surprise here. With the exceptions of such pro-gun actors as Charlton Heston, currently serving as president of the NRA, Tom Selleck, and some others, Hollywood has provided massive celebrity support for the gun-control movement for the past three decades or so. But the spate of school shootings over the past few years has encouraged a considerable public reaction against the mindless violence found in the movies, music, video games, etc., that the entertainment industry has been producing for teen consumption.

While reformers have long argued that movies, comic books, and other manifestations of popular culture have a negative impact on the young, that past popular culture was positively pacifistic compared to what is currently available. And the actions of several of the teen monsters who have shot their classmates and teachers is so similar to scenarios depicted in movies, rap songs, and video games that it has become increasingly difficult to ignore the possibility that popular culture has greatly influenced their actions. So the entertainment industry in general, and Hollywood in particular, has been taking much heat from the public and politicians, liberals as well as conservatives. Even Bill Clinton, in spite of the strong support through thick and thin that he has received from Hollywood, has felt obliged to order a government study of the possible connections between popular-cultural violence and real teen violence. And the entertainment industry has predictably responded to the criticism it is receiving by attempting to deflect it to the favorite target of those in enlightened mainstream-media and politically-liberal circles when it comes to placing blame for our high violent crime rate—the easy access to guns in this country.

Extreme popular-cultural violence can't explain our violent teens, Jack Valenti and other industry spokespersons argue at every opportunity, because if it did other countries such as England and Japan that consume our popular culture, or even more violent popular cultures of their own, would have teens as, or more, violent than ours. Since these other countries consume violent popular culture but don't have our violence problems, our violent popular culture can't be blamed for our violent teens. So what do we have that other countries don't have that explains why we're violent and they're not? We have guns and easy access to them, the Valentis and O'Donnells are quick to point out, and they are seldom challenged through the mainstream media.

But if easy access to guns promotes violence, what is the explanation for the negligible violent-crime rates, teen or otherwise, in such countries as Switzerland and Israel whose citizens have very easy access to guns, or for that matter, the much lower violent-crime rates in this country from the 1940s through the middle 1960s when it was far easier to get guns than it has been since 1968? In Switzerland, a nation of approximately 7 million people that relies on a well-organized militia for its protection, practically every household containing a male between the ages of 20 and 50 possesses at least one *government-issued true assault rifle* and ammunition for it.

These rifles, unlike what are misleadingly referred to as "semiautomatic assault weapons" in this country, can be fired not only semiautomatically (one shot per trigger pull) but automatically (firing as long as the trigger is held back). In the United States, the civilian possession of full-automatic firearms (machine guns) has been strictly regulated by the federal government since 1934, some states ban them, and no new machine guns have been allowed to enter civilian circulation legally since 1986. The Swiss government has put about 600,000 such guns in homes across Switzerland. Militia officers, who serve until age 55, are issued semiautomatic pistols, and militiamen, once retired, keep their rifles or pistols. In addition, as a nation of target shooters and hunters, the Swiss commonly own sporting rifles, shotguns, and handguns. Only handguns require an easy-to-get permit to purchase and possess but about half of Switzerland's cantons don't even require a permit to carry a concealed handgun. And the Swiss can get permits to own anti-aircraft and artillery pieces.

In Israel, a nation of about 4.5 million people, though no right to keep and bear arms is recognized, and gun controls seem very strict, gun density is very high. Permits to own handguns for self-defense are easy to get and the police actually encourage Israelis who own handguns to carry them so that they can't easily fall into the wrong hands and can be used for defense against terrorists. In addition, many government-owned military firearms are in circulation throughout Israel because of mandatory military and reserve requirements, and policies that require soldiers and reservists to take their guns home on leave with them. Students on trips into the countryside must be accompanied by teachers or parents armed with firearms (including Uzi submachine guns and true assault rifles) checked out from local police stations, and such firearms are also issued to police volunteers that include 16- to 18-year-old high school students.

The homicide rates for both Switzerland and Israel run about one per 100,000, not counting "political," or terrorist, homicides in the latter nation. England/Wales and Japan with their very strict gun controls have homicide rates in the same range, again not counting "political" homicides in Britain. Homicide rates for other European nations with strict gun controls such as Denmark, Hungary, and Luxembourg range from around three to almost five per 100,000. The Israeli suicide rate runs about eight per 100,000, and though the Swiss rate is much higher, around 24 per 100,000, it is in the same range as the rates of France, Denmark, Belgium, and

Austria, and much lower than the Hungarian and Romanian rates of about 40 and 66 per 100,000 respectively.

In the United States, the suicide rate ranging around 12.5 per 100,000 is considerably lower than those of the nations of continental Europe, most of which have strict gun controls, but the homicide rate hovered around nine per 100,000 from the mid-1970s into the 1990s, dropping to six in 1998. However, from the mid-1940s through the mid-1960s, when there were few restrictions nationally on the acquisition or possession of guns in the United States, the homicide rate ranged around five per 100,000.

Since I remember those relatively peaceful mid-'40s through the mid-'60s very well, I'm both exasperated and amused by claims that easy access to guns accounts for our high violent-crime rate over the past 35 or so years. Prior to passage of the Gun Control Act of 1968, there were *no national age restrictions* on the purchase of guns in the United States. Over most of the country, guns could not only be purchased without background checks or waiting periods, but through the mail. Sporting shotguns, rifles, and handguns could be purchased through the mail from Sears, Roebuck and Montgomery Ward, and gun, outdoor, and men's magazines carried the advertisements of companies that sold military surplus guns from around the world through the mail at bargain prices—rifles (semiautomatic as well as bolt-action), handguns (semiautomatic as well as revolvers), and even semiautomatic 20mm anti-tank rifles. Even the federal government sold surplus US military rifles, carbines, and handguns, including semiautomatics, to the public at bargain prices through the Army's Office of the Director of Civilian Marksmanship (DCM). Just after World War II, the DCM sold bolt-action .30-06-caliber 1917 Enfields (our main World War I battle rifle, which also saw limited service during World War II) for under $10.00 each, and World War II .30-caliber, *semi*automatic carbines could be had for $20 as late as the mid-'60s.

In response to the easy-access-to-guns-promotes-violent-crime argument, the writer of a recent letter to the editor of our local Evansville, Indiana newspaper noted that he purchased his first handgun, a semiautomatic, 9mm German Luger, through the mail when he was 16 years old back in those old days when the violent-crime rate was considerably lower than it is now. At a recent unofficial, annual mini-reunion of my Herrin Township (Illinois) High School class of 1951, the husband of one of my classmates, himself a 1948 graduate, told how one of his *grade school* teachers had once allowed him to keep his .22-caliber rifle in the cloakroom, since he was going hunting after school.

When I was an undergraduate at then-small Southern Illinois University back in the early 1950s, it was not uncommon for male students from small towns or rural areas to keep guns in their on-campus dorm rooms. One of my friends had two .22 rifles and a shotgun decorating his dorm-room wall. I once asked and received permission to fire off a surprise blank from a handgun during a class speech I gave on gun safety, and another time wore that same handgun in a holster as part of my costume for a Western-theme open house at my dorm. A couple of my friends also carried real handguns on that occasion. There were no campus shootings, accidental or otherwise, in those days, and no thefts of guns even though our dorms were flimsy World War II barracks with skeleton-key locks.

I should add that the place that sold the biggest milkshakes in town also sold cheap .22 revolvers of the sort now vilified as "Saturday night specials." And the shooting range of the Air Force Reserve Officer Training Corps rifle team, of which I was a member my senior year, was in the attic of the main classroom building. While serving in the Air Force during the late '50s, I was based at a small radar station near Miles City, Montana and belonged to a civilian gun club in town. Our shooting range was on the second floor of a building in the middle of the business district. One evening, after a shooting session, several of us went to a nearby restaurant and while there took out our handguns and compared them. We didn't even consider the possibility that anyone would be troubled by this display of weaponry, and in fact, no one gave us a second look.

Certainly if there were no guns there would be no gun-related crime. But as Switzerland, Israel, and even various times and places in the United States prove, the mere widespread possession of guns does not in itself promote high rates of violent crime. Even now, after the school shootings in some smaller communities in recent years, American violent crime is primarily the work of urban, underclass black and Hispanic youths, and urban areas have far lower gun densities than do rural and small-town areas. According to figures cited by Florida State criminologist Gary Kleck, 79.7% of American farm households possess guns while only 10.5% of the households of cities of a million or more possess them. And John Lott, of the University of Chicago's law school (now senior research fellow at Yale University Law School), has presented compelling research covering every county in the country indicating that even today the parts of the U.S. that have the most guns have the least violent crime. Consider that Vermont, which requires no permit to carry a handgun concealed, had a 1992 homicide rate of 0.7 per 100,000, and such high-gun-density states as Montana, North Dakota and South Dakota as of 1992 had, respectively, rates of 2.22, 1.9 and 0.6.

For all of the reasons cited above, Hollywood's easy-access-to-guns-promotes-violent-crime argument, doesn't pass muster. But as the standard liberal mantra unquestioned in enlightened and elitist circles, this argument has allowed what Hollywood has done with guns over this period of time to go unexamined. The 1950 movie *Winchester 73* was a western starring Jimmy Stewart as the hero and Stephen McNally as the villain. But in a sense, the star of the movie was its namesake, the very fancy Winchester Model 1873 rifle won in a shooting match by the Stewart character early in the movie, and stolen from him shortly thereafter by his nemesis, the McNally character he had bested. Much was made over that gun, both in the movie by the shooting match participants and onlookers, and during the promotion and opening of the movie when the rifle used in it was put on display. Hollywood in no way presented its star Winchester negatively. In fact, it was presented quite positively as a fine tool that good men would take great pride in owning. And it was a neutral tool that, as the movie demonstrated, could be put to bad use in the hands of a bad man or good use in the hands of a good man.

Skip ahead to 1971 and *Dirty Harry*, the first of several movies in which Clint Eastwood plays an unruly but honest and dedicated cop whose trademark is the huge Smith & Wesson .44 Magnum revolver he carries. Eastwood's S&W is also a fine precision instrument, but the characteristic emphasized in the movie is the damage it can do, or at least, that the moviemaker wants us to think it can do, to the human body. Pointing his revolver at the face of a criminal he has apprehended, Eastwood's Harry informs him that "this is a .44 Magnum, the most powerful handgun in the world, and would blow your head clean off." This gun is not only a tool, it's a very powerful and destructive device, and as such it is menacing even in the hands of a cop who, though unruly, is dedicated to combating criminals.

These two movies come to mind when I think about Hollywood's symbolic transformation of the gun since the '60s. Prior to the mid- to late '60s, Hollywood seldom presented guns themselves as menacing or focused on their destructiveness. Guns were tools that good people, in uniform or otherwise, used to defeat bad people who also had guns but, fortunately, were somewhat less skilled in their use. Besides *Winchester 73,* guns, their inventors, and sharpshooters were celebrated in the titles of such movies as Randolph Scott's *Colt .45* (1950); Gary Cooper's *Springfield Rifle* (1952); Stewart's *Carbine Williams* (1952), and Betty Hutton's musical *Annie Get Your Gun* (1950), and of such 1950s TV westerns as Chuck Connors' *The Rifleman;* James Arness' *Gunsmoke,* and Richard Boone's *Have Gun Will Travel.* Distinctive guns, usually one or two ivory- or stag-handled six-shooters, but sometimes, as in the case of Steve McQueen's *Wanted Dead or Alive* and Connors' *The Rifleman,* altered rifles, served to mark off almost all B-, TV-, and many big-budget-western heroes from those with whom they mingled.

In the 1955 film, *The Desperate Hours,* Fredric March's character comes home from work to find his family held hostage by three escaped convicts. He keeps a semiautomatic pistol in the house for protection, but the cons, already armed with a revolver acquired during their escape, have found it. No issue is made of the fact that a gun was kept in the house for protection, or the fact that the cons acquire it. But toward the end of the movie, when March is sent on an errand by the cons, he acquires a semiautomatic pistol from the police, unloads it, takes it back home with him knowing that he will be searched and the pistol found, hoping that the cons won't check to see if it's loaded, and that reliance on that empty gun will eventually lead to their undoing. Of course, that's what happens, but the interesting point is, given the subject at hand, that here is a movie where a gun kept in the home for protection and an ordinary, modern, urban citizen's knowledge of firearms are simply taken for granted—not an uncommon Hollywood occurrence before the mid-'60s. In *His Kind of Woman* (1951), Robert Mitchum and Vincent Price, the latter playing a ham movie actor who is an avid hunter and owns a number of guns, also as ordinary, modern, urban citizens display enough prowess with guns to best mobster Raymond Burr and his henchmen with little help from comical Mexican provincial police.

By 1975's *Mahogany,* however, the mere proud display of a handgun collection was enough to confirm the spookiness of one of fashion model Diana Ross' admirers, played by Anthony Perkins. And during the '70s and '80s, a number of TV situation comedies (such as *All in the Family*), crime dramas (such as *Night Caller*), and other TV series aired episodes illustrating the alleged dangers associated with ordinary people keeping guns for personal protection. In fact, one TV movie claiming to explore this issue evenhandedly was ominously titled *A Gun in the House.* Needless to say, none of the characters in these TV offerings who armed themselves for their own protection were able to ward off criminal attack successfully—guns were turned on their owners by criminals, or their owners shot the wrong person, etc.

The self-reliant and gun-wise folks of the Old West have been out of favor with Hollywood since the late '60s, though they still show up occasionally in the likes of TV's *Lonesome Dove* (1988) and *Conagher* (1993). *Matewan* (1987), by independent filmmaker John Sayles, *The Milagro Beanfield War* (1988) directed by Robert Redford, and pro-gun director John Milius' *Red Dawn* (1984), all depicted small, 20th-century armed communities fighting off oppression (coal-company goons, a politically-connected land developer, and communist invaders, respectively). *Star Wars* (1977), a George Lucas creation, and its successors have civilians in a "galaxy far, far away" fighting off oppressors with guns and other weapons, and another Lucas creation (1981), archaeologist Indiana Jones, also handles guns well. But since the '60s, modern urbanites and suburbanites—on big and little screen alike—far more often than not have been incapable of gun-assisted self-help and in need of police protection. *In the real world, research indicates that every year there are anywhere from 760,000 to 3.5 million defensive uses of guns by private citizens.*

From the '50s on back, western movie heroes regularly, if unrealistically, disarmed their opponents by shooting guns out of their hands. The hands those guns were shot out of were seldom more than stung, if that, and the guns shot out of those hands suffered no damage at all. In other words, Hollywood regularly ignored the power of guns. For the past three decades or so, however, Hollywood has tended to exaggerate the power of guns. This exaggeration apparently started with *Shane* way back in 1953, when the farmer Jack Palance's villainous gunfighter shoots is lifted off of his feet by the impact of the bullet and slammed back in the mud. It seems to have taken a while for such laws-of-physics-defying nonsense to catch on, but gunshot victims knocked head-over-heels by the impact even of cinema slugs fired from guns far less potent than Dirty Harry's .44 Magnum eventually became standard fare in TV police shows like *Miami Vice* and *Hunter*, and on the large screen as well.

But Hollywood hasn't only transformed guns from neutral tools, useful to good people concerned with protecting themselves and their significant others from bad people, to destructive devices useless and dangerous to ordinary good people who are incapable of handling them safely. It has also transformed those deemed worthy of handling guns. Eastwood critic Pauline Kael has written: "This is no longer the romantic world in which the hero is, fortunately, the best shot; instead, the best shot is the hero." Kael's comment is cited in Richard Schickel's *Clint Eastwood: A Biography,* which though a worshipful tribute to its subject's acting and directorial skills nevertheless offers numerous interesting insights into modern, or even postmodern, popular culture and its consumers.

Schickel notes that sometime during the cultural upheaval in the '60s filmmakers began to realize "that the audience really doesn't care a rap about who shoots whom or why, so long as the matter is handled with—yes—a certain 'panache.'" He continues: "That this revised context to some degree revises the nature of screen heroism, encouraging us to root for our guy on the basis of his superior style, not his heavier moral weight. What could be more subversive to our traditional codes of heroism than the idea that its largest imperative is to style, to cool improvisation in the heat of the deadly moment?" Mister amoral cool himself, James

Bond with his "007 license to kill," preceded Dirty Harry to the big screen by nearly a decade and was followed by a host of imitators. And in the middle '60s came Eastwood's nihilistic spaghetti westerns (made in Italy but popular here) and their imitators.

While Gary Cooper's *Sergeant York* (1941), like the real life York, had to overcome his pacifism before he could kill enemy soldiers, and movie-cowboy heroes prior to the '60s often shot guns out of the hands of villains rather than kill them, post-'60s Bond-type "heroes" joke about killing. And Eastwood apparently spoke not only for himself but for many other '60s and later action stars when he told an interviewer, "I do the stuff (John) Wayne would never do. I play bigger-than-life characters, but I'll shoot a guy in the back. I go by the expediency of the moment."

So has Paul Newman, one of Hollywood's most vociferous and sanctimonious gun prohibitionists. In *Hombre* (1967), Newman's "hero" shoots outlaw leader Richard Boone while the latter, though not carrying a white flag, considers himself in a truce situation, something that no traditional hero would have ever considered doing. Nor would any traditional hero execute even deserving thugs as coolly as Charles Bronson did in his vigilante *Death Wish* movies, starting in 1974. The lid came off in the '60s and cinema killings by "heroes" became casual, cool, remorseless, even humorous, and without moral context. The '90s have given us films like *Basketball Diaries* which depict righteous, disgruntled youths massacring fellow students.

Guns are neither good nor bad; they are inanimate objects, hunks of metal and other durable materials that are developed and used within social-cultural contexts that assign them their meanings and guide the uses to which they're put. Where cultural contexts and intact communities encourage the socially-acceptable use of guns, as is the case in Switzerland, Israel, and still to a great extent in small-town and rural areas of the United States, *even though their possession is widespread,* guns are seldom misused. Where cultures or subcultures encourage the misuse of guns and/ or families or communities are fragmented, as is often the case in underclass urban areas in this country but is more and more the case even in small-town and rural areas, gun possession can prove troublesome.

Storytelling has been a prime socializing tool from the dawn of man to the high-tech present. Through most of man's prehistory and history, the young heard from their elders stories that provided them with maps for living their lives, as families or whole communities gathered around fires in the evening. By the time I came along in 1933, such stories came from public schools and mass-produced popular culture transmitted through mass media as well as from family settings, but in my experience the lessons to be learned from these different story sources in those days generally reinforced rather than undermined each other. That's less likely to be the case for today's young, particularly when it comes to what they learn about guns.

In the United States, many of today's young come from single-parent or fragmented families, and few among those intact urban or suburban families that still manage to monitor the activities of their offspring know much about acceptable gun use to pass on to them. That means that many American youngsters know little or no more about guns than they get from an entertainment industry that caters to the young and their teen culture; an industry that has demonized guns, exaggerated their power, and transformed those popular cultural "heroes" skilled in their use into cynical, cool, amoral killers. This doesn't happen in Switzerland where teenagers are closer to their parents (who know a lot about guns) than to their peers, family and community ties are still strong, and as David Kopel has noted, Rambo guns are owned but Sylvester Stallone's *Rambo* movies and other violent films are banned.

Fort Worth Star Telegram columnist Bill Thompson has written, "We could pile up guns and pipe bombs and hand grenades in front of well-adjusted youngsters all day long, and not one of them would consider grabbing those devices and using them to slaughter teachers and fellow students. What has happened to kids who would do such a thing?" Many things have happened to them, most related to the undermining of family, community, and widely-accepted normative systems by gradual, if uneven, modernization, and now postmodernization that have affected different social-cultural systems in different ways. Cultural elites and the entertainment industry both reflect and promote the normless aspect of this modernizing-to-postmodernizing process. Since literally millions of kids consume the movies, music and games provided them by the entertainment industry, but very few, even of those millions who have easy access to weaponry, go on murderous rampages, it should be obvious that neither the consumption of nihilistic popular culture nor easy access to weapons in and of themselves *cause* any given rampage. But today's entertainment industry tells the young stories to which they would never have been exposed 30-plus years ago. And as isolated as many young people now are from responsible adult input into their lives, it should hardly be surprising that some of the more isolated and resentful ones (spurred on by their craving for certain mass-media-generated celebrity) occasionally act out this nihilism through violent rampages while they're still young or even later in life.

More common fallouts of the current state of society and what Tipper Gore has called its "toxic popular culture" are risky behaviors involving drugs and sex that have been incorporated into adult-free teen culture. There was very easy youth access to guns in the '40s and '50s I experienced, and even grade-school boys commonly carried pocket knives—I started carrying one in the third grade. But there was negligible youth violence. There was no easy access to sex, even though boys and girls were physically equipped then as they are now. I knew of no unwed schoolgirl mothers when I was in high school, but that was before, among other things, the divorce rate zoomed up, unwed opposite-sex cohabitation and unwed mothers became acceptable even in rural areas and small towns, daycare and TV took the place of parents, and schools were transformed into neighborhoodless youth ghettoes, providing fertile environments for the development of entertainment-media-fed teen culture. And drugs were a non-issue, even when I was in college and the military. Such troublesome phenomena, promiscuous sex, drug use, and youth violence—of the middle-class or even the underclass variety—can't be understood separately. They are the troublesome tips of the modernizing-postmodernizing iceberg that have been glamorized by Hollywood and the entertainment industry and made part of socialization stories for the young. Of course, all of this is likely to be lost on the progressive and enlightened entertainment celebrities listed in Handgun Control Inc.'s *USA Today* ad.

SUNDAYS PAST: GUNS, POPULAR CULTURE, FAMILY, AND ME

This is a revised and updated version of an essay originally published as "Sundays Past" in Liberty, December, 2001, *and reprinted in short form as "My Herrin Sundays Past" in the Southern Illinois regional magazine* Springhouse, *Summer, 2003.*

a-Ape!

a-Ape!" The faint cry came from about three blocks up tree-lined 10th Sheet—north, toward the high school. But I knew that it would be getting louder, because it would be coming my way. And as it got louder, it would be accompanied by a rumble that stopped and started again, and became louder itself. Sunday morning was on its way and would soon officially arrive for me. The "a-Ape" was the cry of the paperboy. He was actually yelling "pay-a-per!" but regardless of who he was and as long as there were paperboys to yell it, the front "p" and the end "r" were lost to the listener, even up close, while the added "a" in the middle was loudly emphasized. For years I thought that paperboys, for some mysterious reason known only to them, yelled "a-Ape." The rumble that accompanied him was produced by the iron wheels of the pushcart that carried his assortment of big-city Sunday newspapers over the brick streets of my home town, Herrin, Illinois, then still a coal-mining town of about 10,000, located about a hundred miles southeast of St. Louis and three hundred miles south and slightly west of Chicago. Herrin is in the far south of Illinois, the "other

Illinois" that is neither big-city Chicago nor flat, treeless farm land, an area long known as "Little Egypt," or sometimes, the "land between the rivers"—the Mississippi, the Ohio, and the Wabash.

It was the paperboy who brought me the magic of the Sunday colored comic pages during my childhood—I was born in 1933—and every seven days those colored comics launched a day full of special events for me, events rooted in a different time, that have left me with a special fondness for Sundays, even though times and Sundays have changed. On weekdays, my dad brought the *St. Louis Star-Times* home from work with him in the evening, and I avidly followed its black-and-white comics, but on Sundays my comics' horizon expanded at the same time that it became more colorful. From the paperboy's cart, my folks bought the *Chicago Tribune* and the *Chicago Herald and Examiner,* which became the *Herald American* in 1939. Between them these papers carried not only colored editions of some of the daily strips, such as *Terry and the Pirates,* that I followed in the *Star-Times,* but others, such as *Prince Valiant* and *Flash Gordon,* which didn't appear in daily comic pages at that time.

While I enjoyed many of the actual comical strips, particularly *The Katzenjammer Kids* with its exotic tropical setting, I lived the better-drawn adventure strips, particularly *Prince Valiant, Flash Gordon, Terry and the Pirates,* and, to a lesser extent, the western *Little Joe.* No sooner did my mom neaten up the various sections of the Sunday paper than I had the comics out again. I not only read those comics, in those pre-television days I devoured them, returning to them throughout the day to admire their artwork (drawing was one of my favorite pastimes during my grade school days) and to become absorbed in the settings and situations depicted.

Prince Valiant transported me to comic artist Harold Foster's imaginative blending of the 5th-century world that might have produced a real King Arthur, with 13th-century Arthurian legend, and in doing so did more to foster my lifelong interest in history than any history course I've ever taken. My eventual recognition that jousting knights and Roman legionnaires didn't occupy the same historical time slot came to trouble me some, but *Prince Valiant* was still a magnificent strip with its depictions of grand vistas, battle scenes, Camelot, and Valiant's bejeweled Singing Sword. Some panels stuck in my memory for decades. Milton Caniff's *Terry and the Pirates* transported me to the exotic Far East of the 1930s and 1940s, and I still remember that bright red P-51 Mustang flown by Terry's World War II buddy, Hotshot Charley. And those canyons turned purple and red by western sunsets still come to mind when I think of *Little Joe,* a lesser-known creation of politically controversial *Little Orphan Annie* cartoonist Harold Gray.

Buck Rogers appeared, as I recall, in both the *St. Louis Globe Democrat* and the *St. Louis Post-Dispatch,* papers that my maternal and paternal grandparents, respectively, bought from the paperboy on Sunday. This strip, along with Alex Raymond's *Flash Gordon,* extended the domain of good guy/bad guy conflict into space and the gleaming cities of other worlds. Fantastic! But I can still remember the disappointment I experienced when a 1947 issue of the aviation magazine *Air Trails,* one of my favorite magazines at the time, carried an article describing the planets of our solar system as they had come to be known even then—uninhabited gas balls or barren rocks. So much for the romance of space, though the "flying saucer" phenomenon that took root that same year has helped even a skeptic like me to cling to some of those romantic associations.

The worlds of these and other of my favorite adventure strips, such as *The Phantom, Buzz Sawyer, Dick Tracy, Smilin'Jack, Brick Bradford, Tim Tyler's Luck,* and *The Lone Ranger,* were inhabited by bold, honorable men who used their wits, strength, and skill with weapons to fight clearly-defined evil. Many of these strips were also inhabited by beautiful women, often rather formidable themselves, who were loyal to the heroes, who were loyal to them. There was no doubt about the masculinity of the comic heroes or the femininity of their heroines in those days, before it became politically incorrect to be concerned about either, nor was there any apology for violence done in the cause of justice. Newspaper comic heroes weren't bullies—they fought when they had to fight, often reluctantly, but always on the side of clearly defined right.

If I'm not mistaken, it was my third-grade teacher, a nice lady I still remember fondly, who one Monday morning asked our class something about our church attendance the previous day. While such a question asked in a public school in practically any community nowadays would trigger civil-liberties concerns about maintaining a wall of separation between church and state, in small-town southern Illinois in 1941 or 1942 it had no such effect. The question did give me some anxious moments, however, because I come from a non-religious family. Casting about for an acceptable response, when it came my turn to answer, I told the teacher that I read the comics on Sunday mornings and that was that. I was just trying to get the teacher off my back, so to speak, but in a way I received from those colorful panels a secularized version of the morality my classmates learned in Sunday school. Their messages about right and wrong reinforced the messages I got from my family, and they've left me impressed by the power of popular culture—so impressed, in fact, that I cringe every time I think of the impact that today's popular culture must be having on the young.

Religion then, did nothing to make Sundays special for me. All of my grandparents and a number of their relations and friends, at least ten families in all, not only dropped out of the Roman Catholic Church, but out of religion entirely when they came to the United States from the Piedmont region of northern Italy in the early 1900s. When I was young I took my family's lack of religion for granted; consequently, I made no effort to discover why they had abandoned it. I've since found that for a number of reasons it was not uncommon for Italian immigrants to leave Catholicism or religion altogether—the secularizing impact of the European industrial and political revolutions of the 18th and 19th centuries on north Italians, the south Italian peasant's perception of the Church as oppressive, the Irish control of the Church in this country, etc. The Church was even aware of its "Italian problem." Anyway, both of my grandfathers were Masons, albeit as members of what a Masonic uncle once told me are called "clandestine lodges." Apparently that was because local lodges of this international brotherhood wouldn't accept Italian-immigrant members in the early 1900s. At least, that's the story as I remember it. I have no idea how my grandfathers, or my uncle, for that matter, reconciled their membership with the Masonic insistence that their members believe in a supreme being.

Number 7

So after the arrival of the comics, the next event that marked off Sundays as special for me was Sunday dinner. We ate all of our other meals in the kitchen, but on Sundays and holidays our big meal was eaten in the dining room. The time varied somewhat because it depended on when my dad got home from work. As the manager of the largest hotel in town, the 99-room (advertised as 100 rooms) Ly-Mar (named after its owners, Lyerla and Marlow), he worked every day of the week, including holidays. Leaving home at about 7:15 a.m., he'd walk four blocks to the hotel (my folks never owned a car), and he'd come back home at about 12:30 p.m. on his lunch break. That break lasted until about 3:00 p.m. and he'd get back home in the evening at about 7:30. He came straight home every night.

Whenever he got home on his break, my mom, in my opinion an excellent cook, would have the meal ready, and on Sundays that meal was always a little special. The main dish might be as American as baked chicken, meat loaf, or some kind of roast, or it might be north-Italian *polenta, risotto,* or spaghetti with or without meat sauce. *Polenta* is a cornmeal mush, and in my family it was always accompanied by some kind of meat or fish fixed in a tomato-based sauce, or *bagna.* The meat and sauce are poured over the mush. The fish was always cod filets, but the meat could be chicken, rabbit, squirrel, beef, or, my favorite, an Italian pork sausage that we Piedmontese call *sautissa* and our Italian neighbors from Lombardy call *luganiga.* I'm not certain of the *sautissa* spelling, but I've seen it as *salsiccia* on restaurant menus and as *salsiccia lucana* in an Italian cookbook. *Risotto* is Italian rice, and in my family it was also fixed with tomato sauce, but the Lombards often fix it with saffron. Side dishes ranged from mashed or baked potatoes to breaded eggplant or breaded cauliflower, and my mom always fixed green beans and green peas with tomato sauce. And there was often a special fresh-baked cake or pie for dessert.

What we did between the time we finished Sunday dinner and the time that my dad went back to work varied considerably from one week to the next. If my parents were involved in remodeling our house, and they often were, my dad, a self-taught master of remodeling skills, might change clothes and work on that project until he had to wash up, change again, and go back to work. If no project was in progress, but the weather left something to be desired, he might take a nap while my mom (with my help as I got older) cleaned up after dinner. But on very special Sundays, the three of us would take a walk out in the country to or beyond the No. 7 coal mine area on the east edge of town—*and we always had one or more guns with us.*

These "walks" were really recreational shooting expeditions, and at an early age, as naturally as taking my first step, I fired a gun for the first time. I may have been six or even younger. The gun would have been a .22, either my dad's Remington Model 34 bolt-action rifle or his Colt Woodsman semiautomatic pistol—probably the former. I do know that though I wasn't allowed to go shooting by myself until I was a junior in high school, by the time that I was twelve I had fired, under parental supervision, not only the .22 rifles and pistols with which I had been introduced to shooting, but a 9mm Luger, a 1903 Colt .38ACP, a commercial Colt 1911A1 .45ACP, a Colt Peacemaker .45, a Winchester 1892 .25-20, an M1 30-caliber carbine, and a 1903A3 Springfield .30-06, among other handguns and rifles.

Among my earliest memories, back when I was no older than three, are those of my dad cleaning his pistols. When I was four or five I banged up my head in a fall, and I clearly remember that to calm me down as my mom patched me up, my dad allowed me to handle the tiny Colt .25 semiautomatic pistol (unloaded) that he often carried to work with him. I had two BB guns, one rubber-band powered, by the time I was six, and I received a powerful Benjamin for my ninth birthday, though it was several years before I could use the airguns without supervision. Colt, Remington, Hi-Standard, joined in later years by Smith & Wesson, Harrington & Richardson, Ruger, and others, were household names, music to my ears. I associated these names not only with precision instruments beautifully sculpted out of steel and other durable materials, but with wholesome family rec-reation and the outdoors, and with the actions of popular-cultural and real heroes, past and contemporary. And many of these guns were semiautomatics, a type of action that the mainstream media seem to have only recently discovered, even though it has been in common civilian use since around 1900.

While I tend to remember our shooting expeditions as Sunday activities, we occasionally went shooting on week-days. Probably my most memorable weekday shoot took place a day or so before my dad had to report for his draft physical during World War II. I was nine or ten at the time, and thinking less of the dangers that he might face in the military than I was of the fact that he would be away from home, which he never was when he wasn't working. To cheer me up, my parents took me shooting, and as I recall, the gun we used that day was an old Colt Single Action Army .45-caliber revolver, a favorite in both the Old West and Hollywood westerns, and also a favorite of one of my World War II heroes, General George S. Patton. Patton's Colt had ivory grips (not pearl, as was often reported) and was silver-plated and engraved—much fancier than ours. As it turned out, my dad, a very robust man who went on to mow his large lawn with a motorless lawnmower until he was 91, failed his physical due to a three-week bout with vertigo he had suffered several years earlier, and I can still remember how happy my mom and I were when he sent us the news.

After the war my dad sold that old Colt and a .41-caliber mate of the same model, one made in 1887 and the other in 1892, for about 25 or 30 dollars each. Since he had bought them for three dollars each from a young man who was leaving for the military, and no one was interested in these old guns at the time, that seemed like too big a profit to pass up to someone from an immigrant, mining-family background who had experienced the Depression. Who knew that those old Colts would now bring at least $2,000 apiece? But I wouldn't want to sell them if I still had them.

When we went shooting we carried our gun or guns in plain sight as we walked the three blocks or so to the edge of town. From the late 1930s to the late 1950s there were no highly publicized anti-gun sentiments, and gun ownership was then and still is widespread, accepted, and even honored in rural and small-town America. Yet though my home town and area had experienced labor, Ku Klux Klan, and bootlegger wars during the decade before I was born, it had become a very peaceful place by the time I came along. Even the violence of the 1920s, which included the massacre of strike breakers and mine guards by striking miners that made my home town infamous nationally (the Herrin Massacre), and cemented my county's nickname (Bloody Williamson), had been factional rather than random, and rooted in economic and/or cultural ("native"/immigrant) conflict. Though I and many of my high-school classmates came from homes that possessed guns, no one took a gun to school to cause trouble. Boys commonly carried pocket knives, (I started carrying one in the third grade), but they were never pulled in schoolyard scuffles. Drugs were unknown.

The area around No. 7 mine where we went shooting was hardly pristine wilderness. But with its mine ponds and crisscrossing railroad tracks—Illinois Central, Missouri Pacific, Chicago, Burlington and Quincy—steel railroad bridges, quaint arched timber automobile bridge, and its surrounding fields and patches of woods, some swampy, it nevertheless was a combination of the Wild West and wild Africa to me. It was a place for adventure and even of natural beauty, in spite of its industrial encroachments, and I couldn't get enough of it with its red sumac in the fall, golden-brown (or sometimes white) fields and bare branches in the winter, spring pastels, and even in the stifling heat and humidity of summer. Heat and humidity didn't even seem stifling before air-conditioning became common. In later years, the mine pond became so polluted by a washing machine plant (at which I worked in a white-collar job after my Air Force active-duty days) that it actually *caught fire* at least once.

We seldom strayed too far from the railroad tracks on our walks/shooting expeditions, and when we found a tin can or other suitable target we'd set it up against an embankment and blast away at it. My dad and I did most of the shooting, though my mom, not a shooter but approving of our interests in guns, would often take a few shots. As I got older, she left these shooting expeditions to my dad and me. Though I never timed our walks, they probably ran not much more than an hour because they had to be fitted in between Sunday dinner and the time my dad had to go back to work, and time had to be allowed for cleanup and clothes changes. And before he went back to work or that evening, time had to be taken to clean whatever gun or guns we had used.

Sunday Matinees

After my dad went back to work and the dinner dishes had been washed and leftovers put away, my mom and I would almost always go to the movies on Sunday afternoons. And in those days, going to the movies on Sundays was to most people, including us, a dress-up occasion. I've always felt much closer to my family than to my peers and I was quite shy through my grade school years, so although I had neighborhood friends around my age, when I was small I very much enjoyed going to the Sunday movies with my mom. But by going to the movies on Sundays, a practice that I continued even after I struck out on my own, I was exposed to Hollywood offerings that my friends seldom saw and generally missed the ones that they did see.

Herrin had two movie houses when I was small. The Hippodrome, the first-run theater, was located right across the street in the next block south of the hotel my dad managed and was owned by the hotel owner. After this theater burned in the 1940s and was rebuilt it was renamed "Marlow's" after its owner, who also owned the second-run theater, the Annex. The two theaters were located back-to-back, with an alley separating them—Marlow's facing east on 14th Street as did the hotel, and the Annex facing west on Park Avenue, our main street.   The Annex building remains today, but Marlow's and the hotel became victims of "progress."

While nowadays movies that draw well at the box office may be shown for months at the same theater, that wasn't the case in my hometown, and I suspect elsewhere, through the 1950s. On Sundays, the first-run theater had a matinée, and once the proceedings started, the single major Hollywood feature, previews of coming attractions, newsreel, animated cartoon, and selected short subjects repeated without lengthy interruption until the theater closed late in the evening. The same major film would be shown again a couple of times on Monday evening—no matinée. On Tuesday evening two new movies, both of the low-budget "B" variety, would be shown, and this same double feature would be offered again on Wednesday evening. A fresh B double feature would come to the theater on Thursday evening and be held over on Friday before being replaced by yet another double feature on Saturday, a matinée day that almost always included a B western or serial for the kids. So while most children my age were watching B adventures starring Gene Autry, Roy Rogers, or Hopalong Cassidy on Saturday afternoons, on Sunday afternoons my mom and I were watching Hollywood's biggest names and the latest of what passed for adult fare in those days. And I mean the latest.

When I scanned the entertainment sections of the St. Louis and Chicago newspapers back in the 1940s, I never ceased to be amazed that our small-town theater got the major Hollywood pictures at least as soon as did the big-city theaters. In fact, I think that some reached us before they got to the cities. My favorites were the big-budget pictures featuring frontiersmen, military heroes, pirates, knights, swordsmen, and other adventurers.

The swashbuckling Errol Flynn was my favorite actor from the late 1930s through the middle 1940s, and his Elizabethan *The Sea Hawk* (1940), and three westerns, *Dodge City* (1939), *Virginia City* (1940), and particularly, *They Died With Their Boots On* (1941), like the comic strip *Prince Valiant,* fostered my interest in history, even though I eventually discovered that their historical accuracy left much to be desired. *They Died With Their Boots On* was a romanticized and highly imaginative depiction of Custer's last stand, but it left a lasting impression on my eight-year-old mind. For weeks after I saw it, I played Custer in our front yard, equipped with my favorite frontier-style cap pistol, the wooden copy of Prince Valiant's broadsword that my dad had made for me, and a 7th Cavalry guidon I made from one of my mom's sheets turned dish towel. That movie made me a lifelong Custer and Little Big Horn buff, and "Garyowen," the 7th's marching song, still triggers my martial spirit. Garyowen, incidentally, isn't someone's name but Gaelic for Owen's Garden, which is a suburb of Limeric, Ireland. Yes, I know that Custer is no longer politically correct, but interestingly enough, in *They Died With Their Boots On,* greedy whites with political pull rather than the Indians who killed Custer and his men were portrayed as the villains.

Another Sunday movie that impressed me mightily and influenced my solitary play adventures for some time after I saw it was *Jesse James* (1939), starring Tyrone Power as Jesse and Henry Fonda as his brother Frank. In this movie, Jesse (portrayed as a good man who had been driven to become an outlaw by greedy exploiters) was equipped with two six shooters, one with plain grips, the other with ivory grips, the former a Colt and the latter a Smith & Wesson, I discovered in later years. So, gun enthusiast that I'd already become, when I played Jesse I selected just the right cap pistols from my well-cared-for collection. Unlike the real revolvers Power used in the movie, my two Jesse cap pistols were identical *except* for the fact that one of them had black-painted metal grips while the other had *white* Bakelite grips. These two cap pistols with Hollywood-Jesse-appropriate grip colors would accompany me to my maternal grandparents' house, where I'd use two stiff-backed living-room chairs pulled together seat-to-back with a throw rug tossed over them to make what to me was a reasonable facsimile of a train to rob in the name of justice.

My early familiarity with and interest in guns provided me with a very vivid link to movies (particularly westerns) featuring heroes who used guns, and these movies in turn helped reinforce my interest in guns and my linking them to things heroic. In the 1940 *Jesse James* sequel *The Return of Frank James,* when Henry Fonda's Frank, living as an honest farmer under an assumed name, learned of Jesse's assassination, he retrieved his revolver from its hiding place in his barn before setting out to avenge his brother. With the assistance of a second viewing sometime in the late 1940s, the symbolism of that scene and the carved grips on his revolver were etched in my memory. Joel McCrea's *Union Pacific* (1939) was memorable to me in large part due to the pair of stag-handled Colts he carried. The scene that stuck with me from my initial viewing of *Gone With the Wind* (1939) was Vivien Leigh's Scarlett O'Hara dispatching a threatening Union deserter with the long-barreled Remington revolver that Clark Gable's Rhett Butler had given her. One of my Detroit cousins still remembers how when he, his sister, and I went to the movies during their visits, if the wrong guns were being used for the time and place being depicted, I'd always point out that fact to them.

Other Sunday rnatinée offerings during my childhood were war movies like Gary Cooper's *Sergeant York* (1941) and *For Whom the Bell Tolls* (1943), costume adventures like Fonda's *Drums Along the Mohawk* (1939) and Douglas Fairbanks Jr's *The Corsican Brothers* (1942), and comedies like Bud Abbott and Lou Costello's *Buck Privates* (1941) and Bob Hope and Bing Crosby's *Road to Morocco* (1942). And there was a mixed bag of many others: Humphrey Bogart and Ingrid Bergman's *Casablanca* (1942), Judy Garland's *Wizard of Oz* (1939), and Crosby and Fred Astaire's *Holiday Inn* (1942), which introduced the classic song that began as a World War II favorite, "White Christmas."

Along with these and other well-remembered movies that we saw on Sunday afternoons were many soap-operaish romances (dare I call them "women's movies"?) that I've long ago forgotten, but that I suspect may have helped foster a romantic and sentimental streak in me. But then again, practically all adult movies in those days, not only the soap operas, musicals, and comedies, were love stories, and love wasn't synonymous with sex. Rugged frontiersmen or cops courted their ladies at the same time that they dealt with villains, and brave soldiers, as they faced enemies on bat-tlefields far away, thought about their loyal wives or sweet-hearts back home for whom they were fighting and would gladly give their lives. Men and women came together in these movies because they loved each other, not because they lusted after each other, a distinction that's now often derided when not altogether forgotten in Hollywood and other popular cultural centers.

But like the comic-strip heroes of the time, the movie heroes of my childhood mentioned above, and even those of my on-my-own-at-the-movies adolescence were a special breed. I'm referring to screen personas, not to the actors who played those heroes, though some actors who often played heroic characters seem to have been decent, honorable men themselves. The John Wayne of director John Ford's cavalry trilogy *Fort Apache* (1948), *She Wore a Yellow Ribbon* (1949), and *Rio Grande* (1950), the Joel McCrea of *Buffalo Bill* (1944) and *The Virginian* (1946), the Tyrone Power of *Captain From Castile* (1947), *Prince of Foxes* (1949), and *The Black Rose* (1950), the Gregory Peck of *Twelve O'Clock High* (1949) and *The Gunfighter* (1950), the Gary Cooper of *Unconquered* (1947), the Stewart Granger of *King Solomon's Mines* (1950), the Van Johnson and others of *Battle Ground* (1949), and many others were brave and tough, but they were also chivalrous gentlemen and decent human beings with a sense of humor as well as a sense of honor. In spite of their strength and/or skill with weapons, these fictional heroes fought only reluctantly, never took unfair advantage of their villainous and formidable opponents, and always protected the weak (kids, women, and the elderly). Villains cheated; heroes didn't, though if the good guys were greatly outnumbered, they could honorably use trickery to overcome their numerical disadvantage. Even John Wayne's crusty, driven rancher in *Red River* (1948) began and ended the movie as a proper John Wayne character. And any day I'll take that John Wayne screen persona over the sullen, menacing, anti-heroic, killing-machine, screen persona that Clint Eastwood perfected in his 1960s "spaghetti westerns" and later cop movies, and that to a certain extent even contaminates, in my opinion, his otherwise admirable *The Outlaw Josey Wales*

(1976). Needless to say, I'm no fan of Eastwood's Academy Award-winning *Unforgiven* (1992), that was such a smash hit with the critics precisely because it was so anti-heroic, morally ambiguous, and non-traditional.

As with our shooting expeditions, our movie-going when I was a kid wasn't always a Sunday pastime. On *very rare* occasions my mom and I would be able to talk my dad into going to a movie after he finished work. Westerns were the best bait, and that was the case with Robert Taylor's *Billy the Kid* (1941). Rather than my mom and I seeing it on Sunday afternoon, the three of us saw it on Monday evening. As with all Hollywood biographical efforts of the time, *Billy the Kid* left much to be desired in the historical-accuracy department, but it was beautifully filmed in color, and the way movies look (scenery and costumes) and sound (the music of the sound track) as much or more than their story lines have always made them memorable to me.

With regard to sound, the tune "Alexander's Ragtime Band" left me with a fondness for the movie by the same name, starring Tyrone Power and Alice Faye (1938), long after I had forgotten its story. "As Time Goes By" brings to my mind Bogart and Bergman's *Casablanca,* and "Moonlight Becomes You" carries me back to Hope, Crosby, and Dorothy Lamour in *Road to Morocco.* But I always found westerns directed by John Ford, with their Monument Valley settings and traditional-music-permeated soundtracks, "The Girl I Left Behind Me," "Garyowen," "She Wore a Yellow Ribbon," "The Yellow Rose of Texas," "Lorena," and many others, particularly impressive in the looks and sound department. The music of a time and place has always carried me back to that time and place.

What my mom and I did after the Sunday matinée depended on what time we got out. Those were the days of "This is where we came in." People commonly entered the movie when they got there, not necessarily at the beginning of the feature, and they stayed until they had seen what they had missed. I don't recall ever seeing a movie from its beginning back then, but we always stayed until it got to the part "where we came in," and sometimes beyond. If getting to a movie late, or a long movie, or watching part of a movie over again put us out at about 7:00 PM, when my dad could sometimes start for home on Sunday evening, we'd drop by the hotel to pick him up and walk home together.

Though I took the hotel my dad managed for granted when I was young, it was sort of a glamorous place with a cool, spacious lobby furnished with comfortable stuffed chairs and divans. My dad came over from Italy when he was three, and he and his folks lived in Herrin for a short while before they moved to New Mexico Territory, where they lived from 1910 to about 1917. He started working at the hotel at age 17 in 1923 and became its manager in 1925, a position he held until the hotel closed in 1963. That was right in the middle of Herrin's wild days—1923 was the year that the Ku Klux Klan came to Williamson County and the year after the Herrin Massacre—and all of "Bloody Williamson's" marquee players—S. Glenn Young, Ora Thomas, the Shelton brothers, and Charlie Birger, among them—were in and out of the Ly-Mar at one time or another. Young, a former revenuer and Texas Ranger (allegedly), who wore a Smoky hat and puttees and packed a pair of pearl-handled Colt 1911 .45s in tied-down holsters suspended from crossed gun belts, led Klan raids enforcing Prohibition, more or less, and literally took over Herrin at one time. He and his wife were living at the Ly-Mar at the time he was killed in a Hollywood-style shootout with Thomas, a deputy sheriff who had gang connections and was killed in the same fight—possibly by Young. My dad always said that both Young and his wife were always nice to the hotel staff, though a couple of years earlier Young and his Klansmen had raided my paternal grandparent's house and my dad had to crawl under the house to throw out the homebrew hidden there. He apparently didn't remember my dad from that incident.

The Shelton brothers, Carl (who packed a pearl-handled Colt Frontier Model, or sometimes, a Luger), Big Earl, and Bernie (who favored a Colt 1911 .45), were Wayne County farm boys who came to control downstate organized crime in Illinois so completely that even Al Capone left them alone. Birger, a Jew who came to this country from Russia when he was a child and later served as a cavalryman on the northern Great Plains in the early 1900s, led a rival gang and was the last person publicly hanged by the state of Illinois. A family friend owned a Colt New Service .38-40 that had belonged to Birger. In that environment, no wonder my dad packed heat—a Mauser 1910 .32ACP or a Colt 1903 .38ACP, but by the peaceful time I came along he carried either a Colt 1903 .32ACP or the .25 I mentioned above. When I was a kid and often heard stories about my home turf's old days from my parents and other family members and friends, I couldn't understand how my peaceful hometown had been so wild when they were young. But it was, as a number of books have related—noted Lincoln historian Paul M. Angle's *Bloody Williamson: A Chapter in American Lawlessness,* Gary DeNeal's *A Knight of Another Sort: Prohibition Days and Charlie Birger,* Taylor Pensoneau's *Brothers Notorious— The Sheltons—Southern Illinois' Legendary Gangsters,* Bill

Nunes' *Southern Illinois, An Illustrated History,* and Donald Bain's *War in Illinois: An Incredible True Story from the Roaring Twenties* among them.

Hotel guests by the time I came along were often famous rather than infamous, ranging from Illinois governors, including two-time Democratic presidential candidate Adlai E. Stevenson, to practically every big band from the golden age of the Big Bands—Harry James, Tommy and Jimmy Dorsey, Guy Lombardo, Kay Kyser, Lawrence Welk, Vaughn Monroe, Stan Kenton, Wayne King, Woody Herman, Benny Goodman, Xavier Cugat, and many others. These bands performed at White City Park, once a Herrin institution also owned by the hotel owner. White City Park's ballroom allegedly drew fun-seekers from a 150-mile radius (an area reaching up to central Illinois and into Missouri, Indiana, Kentucky, Tennessee, and Arkansas) to its Saturday evening dances.

I never saw the inside of that ballroom (now demolished), which was located on the northwest side of town. And though I enjoyed the music of many of those bands, and I often saw them in the movies, it never occurred to me that I should try to get the autographs of any of their leaders or more famous musicians and singers. Their music lingers in my memory, however. "You'd Be So Nice To Come Home To," "Deep Purple," "Where Or When," "My Reverie," "Among My Souvenirs," 'That Old Feeling," "To Each His Own," and other love ballads made a lasting impression on me even when I was a kid too young to appreciate what they were all about. Then there were such silly songs as "Mairzy Doats," and "Chickery Chick." Compare these to much of the "music" today's kids are going to remember.

If the weather was pleasant, we sometimes window-shopped along Park Avenue, our main street, before we walked home. But most of the time we'd be out of the movie long before my dad could leave work, so my mom and I would go on home and I'd listen to radio comedies like *The Jack Benny Program* and *The Edgar Bergen/Charlie McCarthy Show* until he came in.

Once my dad came home from work on Sunday evening, we would eat supper, usually leftovers from our main midday meal. Eating out was not an option for my family in those days, though I do remember a few occasions when we had barbecue sandwiches brought home from the small bar and grill across from the hotel. After supper we'd visit my grandparents, who lived one house from each other one block east of us on 9th Street. Due east of us, 7th Street was the last street before the fields and mine pond that separated our neighborhood in town from the No. 7 mine area.

Since we had no washing machine in those days, we'd carry our dirty laundry over to my maternal grandparents' house on Sunday evening so that my mom and her mom could do a combined washing in her mom's washer on Monday morning. My mom often took time out from her own busy schedule to help her folks, particularly in the spring when they raised cabbage, pepper, and tomato plants in their backyard hotbeds. To supplement their miners' income, my grandparents sold those plants for transplanting at prices that now seem incredibly low, given the work put into raising them: cabbage plants for a nickel a dozen, tomato and pepper plants for 15 cents a dozen or a quarter for three dozen, and tomato plants for 50 cents per 100, once the farmers started buying them late in the season.

We carried our laundry in pillow cases, and once I was big enough to carry them, it was my proud duty to do so. I can still remember the smell of coal smoke in the air from the neighborhood chimneys as we walked the one block east and most of a block south to my maternal grandparents' house on crisp winter evenings. During warm weather we'd pass neighbors sitting on their porches, as was common before air-conditioning and television encouraged people to stay indoors. So there often were brief conversations with neighbors along the way. Practically any evening during warm weather, my maternal grandparents' front porch was the most popular gathering place for several of the neighborhood ladies of their generation. They would sit and gossip or talk about the old country while swishing away mosquitoes with small branches stripped from the maple trees in the front yard.

For blocks around, most of our neighbors were north-Italian immigrants (generally Piedmontese or Lombard) or their offspring, though there were a couple of Syrian/Lebanese families, a second or third-generation German family, a first-generation Welsh family, and a scattering of Southerners whose ancestors had come from the British Isles. So I grew up around many people who felt much more comfortable speaking Piedmontese or Lombard dialects than they were speaking English. I never learned to speak these Italian dialects, I'm sorry to say, but I could understand them as well as I could understand English. When my cousins would come down from Detroit for summer vacations, the high point of my summers, I would translate for them the adult conversations in Piedmontese or Lombard our parents, grandparents, and other grown-ups would be carrying on.

After we had deposited the laundry at my maternal grandparents' house, we visited with them for a while before we started back home, stopping for a short visit with my paternal grandparents (where Piedmontese was generally spoken) along the way. It was during these Sunday evening visits with my grandparents that I followed the adventures of *Buck Rogers,* carried in both of their St. Louis Sunday newspapers, but in neither of the Chicago Sunday newspapers we bought from the paperboy. Once we got home, the specialness of Sunday was over, and there was nothing to do but go to bed at 9:00, whether I wanted to or not. Monday, for nine months of the year at least, meant five more days of school and homework.

Sundays Present

It's been many years since paperboys yelled "a-Ape" and pushed their carts full of big-city Sunday newspapers over the brick streets of my hometown. In fact, many of those streets, including 10th, have been blacktopped. And I now live in Evansville, Indiana, a city of about 120,000, 97 road miles and about a two-hour drive door-to-door from my house to my folks' house where I grew up. Our paper person delivers the *Sunday Evansville Courier & Press* to our front steps the same way that he/she delivers our daily paper. In the late pushcart days, when I still lived with my folks, this newspaper's earlier incarnation was one of the big-city newspapers we bought from the paperboy after the *Chicago Herald American* went out of business, so this Sunday paper helps bridge the gap between my past and my present. And the *Sunday Evansville Courier & Press'* colorful comic pages, like the colorful comics of the past, still provide me with a bright start for Sundays, even though the strips therein are quite different from the strips in the St. Louis and Chicago newspapers of my childhood.

Gone are the beautifully and realistically drawn adventure strips like *Prince Valiant, Flash Gordon*, and *Terry and the Pirates,* though the soap-opera strip *Rex Morgan, M.D.* remains as a less than spectacular example of that drawing tradition. After reading an early draft of this essay, one of my Detroit cousins sent me several comic sections from the Sunday *Detroit Free Press,* which still carries *Prince Valiant* as drawn by Hal Foster's successor. Rather than having a full page to itself, as it did in its heyday, the strip now is crowded on to a page with three or four other strips, and grand panoramas can no longer be depicted. *Rhymes with Orange,* a satirical strip carried in our Evansville newspaper, may have the honor of being the worst-drawn strip to have ever graced a comic page. *Blondie* and *Snuffy Smith* are left over from the old days. Among my current favorites are the political satires *Mallard Fillmore* (which generally reflects my culturally traditional but politically libertarian views) and *Doonesbury* (which often doesn't reflect my views). I always looked forward to the provincial antics of the folks in *Geech,* but it's gone since its creator passed away recently. Then there are the teacher-student antics of the folks in *Funky,* and the family antics of the folks in *Sally Forth, Rose Is Rose, Born Loser, Foxtrot,* and the very politically-correct *For Better or for Worse.* I miss *Calvin and Hobbes,* the fanciful, even philosophical, adventures of a bratty little boy and his stuffed tiger whose creator gave up doing the strip a few years back. But favorites or not, I read all of the strips in the Sunday comic pages, and these colored versions of the black-and-white strips that I read religiously through the rest of the week still help make Sundays special for me, even though other Sunday associations have faded.

My wife has never been fond of Sundays. When she was still working, Sundays were drudgery days used to prepare for the coming work week. But there are other reasons that we haven't developed our own tradition of eating a big Sunday noonday meal in our dining room. Since we didn't have children we've tended to operate on a very flexible schedule, made even more so by our former professions. My wife is a nurse, who, when she worked in a hospital, often worked on Sundays. Both of us have tended to go to bed late and get up late when our schedules have allowed us to do so, and as a former college professor who had late morning classes for many years, my schedule did nothing to discourage this pattern. Consequently, through most of the thirty years of our marriage, both of us have tended to sleep in on Sundays. We have our main Sunday meal at home or out in the afternoon or evening, and it isn't always more special than weekday meals. Recently, we've been going out for brunch around noon and eating a light supper at home.

Things obviously change as we grow up, leave the nest, move around, have to earn our own living, acquire responsibilities, and bring others into our intimate lives through marriage, etc. Rather than a five-minute, block-and-a-half walk to visit my grandparents, it's now a two-hour, 97-mile drive to visit my mom. I make that drive frequently, but my visits are seldom on Sundays because I can't do her banking and run other errands for her on that day. Rather than a fifteen-minute walk out to the country to engage in open-air, recreational shooting free of cost other than the price of ammunition, I now either drive five minutes to an indoor range and pay five dollars for a half-hour of shooting, shut off from the nature that has always enhanced the experience for me, or drive 25 minutes to the outdoor range of the gun club to which I pay 30 dollars a year for membership whether or not I use the range. The 50-minute or so round trip to the club range doesn't encourage me to make that trip often, and I do well to visit it twice a year if at all. I seldom exercise either the indoor or outdoor option on Sundays.

Times change, but there are two cultural disruptions of things that I hold dear and that I associate with Sundays past, movies and guns, that disturb me mightily. While the newspaper comics I read today, Sunday or otherwise, are different from those of my childhood, I still enjoy them very much. Gone are the adventure strips with their heroes and heroines, but most of the strips I currently read are still populated by decent people doing decent domestic things. I wish that I could say the same for the people who populate Hollywood movies nowadays.

Going to the movies was a large part of what made Sundays past special for me, but for a couple of reasons movie-going is seldom a part of my Sundays present. The first and lesser reason is that there's no longer anything special about Sunday movies. Sunday movies during my childhood and adolescence were big-budget movies featuring the top Hollywood stars, and they stayed in town for two days—only one of which, Sunday, had a matinée. Now, though stars like those of days past hardly exist, all movies are big-budget movies, and even the box-office bombs stay in town for several days, while the successful stay for weeks or even months. Therefore, since the cheaper matinees are shown all through the week and I'm retired, there's no particular reason for me to go to a Sunday matinée unless both my wife and I are interested in seeing the same movie. And this brings me to the second and more important reason that movie-going is seldom part of my Sundays present—Hollywood now makes very few movies that either of us want to see and even fewer that both of us want to see.

I'm a sociologist, and as such I'm an extreme cultural relativist. But relativism is an analytical tool for social scientists, not a principle to live by, and in everyday life I make no apologies for being judgmental. Though I'm very familiar with four-letter words and far from a prude, as a product of all that is symbolized by my Sundays past I quite frankly despise the foul-mouthed, promiscuous characters (female as well as male), dysfunctional families, and nihilistic or wussy politically-correct messages that Hollywood has been offering the public for several decades. And the popular-culture-assisted moral ambiguity, well established across the nation during the 1970s, has played havoc with the tough but gentlemanly, decent, honest, and honorable heroes of my Sundays past.

There have been a few big-screen heroic characters of the old sort in movies I've seen during the past decade or so, Daniel Day-Lewis in *The Last of the Mohicans* (1992) and Liam Neeson in *Rob Roy* (1995), among them, but there haven't been enough of them to regularly draw me to the local movie houses at their inflated ticket, popcorn, and drink prices on Sunday or any other day. I've just seen *Open Range* (2003), starring Kevin Costner and Robert Duvall as old-fashioned western heroes. I liked this movie (which could have benefited from period background music), but I waited to see it on a Tuesday afternoon at our second-run cheapie theater for $2.50. Tobey Maguire's character in *Ride With the Devil* (1999) also had much of the old-fashioned hero about him—a decent, likeable guy caught up in the moral ambiguity of the guerrilla war in Missouri during the Civil War. But this movie, after much TV advertisement, seems to have made it to few theaters around the country. I finally rented it at Blockbuster. A few weeks later, I bought it on VHS at Wal-Mart for under five dollars. So I now generally look to American Movie Classics and other cable TV movie channels to rerun my old favorites and put me in touch again with screen characters I can admire, and to occasional made-for-TV gems like TNT's *Monte Walsh* (2003), starring Tom Selleck, and *Conagher* (1993), starring Sam Elliot and Katherine Ross, and CBS's magnificent miniseries *Lonesome Dove* (1988), starring Robert Duvall and Tommy Lee Jones. But though I can still find them occasionally on the big screen, on cable TV, in made-for-TV movies, on VHS sales at Wal-Mart, or in paperback historical westerns by writers like Douglas C. Jones and Richard S. Wheeler, it disturbs me that heroic characters who not too long ago were central to our popular culture and our national mythology have been relegated to the periphery of both, where today's children, fewer of whom are the products of stable families, aren't likely to find them and be impressed by them.

Guns also helped make Sundays past special for me: the guns my folks and I used on our shooting expeditions to No. 7, the guns used by the fictional heroes of many movies and comic strips to fight off oppression and right wrongs, the guns real heroes in movie newsreels were using to win World War II, the guns that were taken for granted as a non-threatening part of the cultural mainstream of rural and small-town America through the late 1950s, and the positive symbolic relationship between all of these guns. But guns are anything but politically correct in influential symbol-manipulating circles nowadays, the same circles that through their popular-cultural offerings—"music," movies, and television—have unthinkingly helped to foster the moral breakdown responsible for high rates of violence that they blame on widespread gun ownership. It does no good to point out to these people that gun-ownership rates in this country have been high when violence rates have been low, and that even now, gun ownership rates are highest where violence rates are lowest. So once-honored guns, like the responsible popular-cultural heroes who once used them, have been stigmatized and pushed to the periphery of the popular culture and the national mythology.

And the urban-oriented middle classes, increasingly unfamiliar with and fearful of guns, refuse to take responsibility for their own safety, and rely on increasingly heavily-armed and militarized police to protect them from vicious underclass thugs, and on professional soldiers rather than citizen soldiers drawn from their own ranks to protect their country from foreign thugs. Not only are popular-culture heroes fewer and farther between, but the urban-oriented middle class seems to be producing fewer individuals willing to take heroic risks in defense of themselves, their families, and their country. And they give no thought to how they'll protect themselves from the armed agents of government if the need ever arises. We seem to be breeding more than our share of feral teenagers, on the one hand, and wimps (many of whom seem to work for the mainstream media when they grow up) on the other. That disturbs me.

Much of the charm of Sundays past for me was obviously rooted in the fact that they were no-school (even during the school year) fun days for a child with no real responsibilities. My mom worked just as hard at home and my dad worked just as hard at the hotel on Sundays as they did any other day, though she usually took time out for the movies in the afternoon, and he might be on the job a half-hour or so less than usual, and both of them occasionally took time off for a recreational shooting expedition in the country.

But fun and lack of real responsibilities don't completely account for my feelings about Sundays past. Sundays were bright days, sun days, even when the sun wasn't shining, because of the convergence of special people, real (my parents and grandparents) as well as fictitious (comic-strip and movie heroes and heroines), special places (my home, my grandparents' homes, the mine area and countryside east of town, the movie theater), and special events (reading the colored comics, meals in the dining room, going shooting, going to the movies, listening to radio comedies, visiting my grandparents). And this convergence of the real and the popular cultural greatly influenced my views on many things, among them what it means to be a member of a loving family, what it means to be a man, what it means to love and be loyal to a woman, and what it means to be a good person and a responsible and patriotic American citizen. I suspect that many Americans prior to the 1960s, though few lived Norman Rockwell perfection, were also likely to experience such positive convergences.

PART III

GUNS AND PEOPLE CONTROL

THE SPIRIT OF NORTHFIELD AND COFFEYVILLE

Originally published in Liberty, *March, 2000, and reprinted as "The Spirit of Northfield and Coffeyville Versus the Consumer of Safety Mentality" in* Gun News Digest, *Spring, 2001.*

The James-Younger gang was a legend in its own time. Most, if not all, of its members had seen guerrilla action in bloody Missouri during the Civil War, and after that conflict they put their war-honed riding and shooting skills to use robbing banks and trains. They were a hard bunch, to put it mildly. But in 1876, they didn't impress the citizens of Northfield, Minnesota.

When Jesse and Frank James, Cole, Bob and Jim Younger, and three other gang members rode into Northfield and set about robbing the local bank, killing an uncooperative cashier and a confused Swede in the process, the locals armed themselves and decimated this gang of hardcases. Of the eight outlaws taking part in the attempted robbery, only Jesse and Frank escaped. The three Younger brothers were shot up and captured by a citizen posse, and the three re-maining gang members were all killed during the attempted robbery or during their escape attempt.

The Dalton brothers, members of another legendary old-time outlaw gang and distant kin of the Youngers, apparently learned nothing from what happened to the Jameses and Youngers at Northfield. In 1892, Bob, Grat and Emmett Dalton, and two other gang members rode into Coffeyville, Kansas intent on robbing not one but two of that community's banks. The locals killed all but Emmett, who was wounded and captured.

Neither Northfield in 1876 nor Coffeyville in 1892 were wild-and-woolly frontier communities of the sort that Hollywood served up to us when it used to make westerns—places where most of the local males paraded around town packing six-shooters. Both towns were peaceful communities located in settled farming areas. Yet when threatened by heavily-armed toughs, their citizens had easy enough access to guns (Coffeyvillians got most of theirs from a hardware store), enough familiarity in their use, and enough spunk to make a stand (several Northfielders without guns threw rocks at the robbers) and to risk casualties (five Coffeyvillians were killed in the fierce shoot-out with the Daltons) in order to destroy formidable outlaw bands.

The much romanticized horse-riding outlaws of the Old West and Midwest have long been absent from the national scene. The most publicized criminal gangs nowadays are much larger than the old outlaw gangs, composed largely of young black or Hispanic males, and mostly operate in big cities. Unlike the old outlaw gangs, these criminal gangs don't stage daring bank robberies and ride off into the shrubbery. Rather, they war against each other over drug turf and, through miscellaneous villainies, make things miserable and dangerous for decent people of various skin colors and ethnicity who live or work within their reach. But these thugs on occasion still encounter the spirit of Northfield and Coffeyville even in urban settings, though that spirit is much under siege in urban-centered political, media and academic circles considered to be enlightened. Two thugs walked into Lance Thomas' Los Angeles watch shop, knocked a customer over the head, and one pointed a gun at Thomas and demanded that he give them his watches. Thomas responded by grabbing his own gun and shooting the armed robber in the face. The thug survived and was sent to prison for five years.

Three and a half months later, two other armed thugs came to rob Thomas. Thomas yelled for his customers to drop to the floor, went for one of his own guns, and called 911 in the middle of the gunfight during which he killed both of his assailants. He was seriously wounded himself—suffering a gunshot wound in the neck and three in the shoulder.

Two years later, a single gunman came to rob Thomas. You guessed it. One guy didn't have a chance against him. He shot and killed the thug. And though Thomas received another neck wound, he was back at work the next day. Finally, with their criminal pride on the line, two members of one of LA's most violent black gangs came to make Thomas, who is white, pay for his prowess. Pretending to open the front door of his shop to leave, they turned, pointed their guns at him and said, "You're dead!" They were wrong. Thomas shot and killed both of them. In four gunfights he suffered and survived five gunshot wounds, but he killed five thugs and wounded a sixth. The citizens of old Northfield and Coffeyville would have been proud of him. But the "enlightened" among his contemporaries really don't know what to make of Thomas. In spite of his spectacular success in protecting himself against armed criminals, it seems that Thomas received no national attention until ABC's October 5, 1994 *Turning Point* special on using guns for self-defense aired. That was five years after his first shoot-out. *Turning Point* let Thomas tell his story: how a friend had advised him to get a gun for protection after other shopkeepers in his area had been robbed and killed; how the first robbery attempt had come not long after he had acquired his first gun; how he added security devices and acquired more guns and practiced with them as the robbery attempts continued; and how he eventually closed up his shop when he heard that the gangs were determined to take revenge on him.

But Don Kladstrup, the ABC reporter interviewing him, seemed genuinely baffled by Thomas' willingness to take on armed robbers, all of whom had had the drop on him. Thomas' reply that he refused "to be a victim of violent crime" made no impression on the reporter, who wanted to know why he hadn't just forked over the loot the robbers were after rather than take human lives and risk his own life. Thomas and Kladstrup seemed to be talking past each other—they were simply on different cultural wavelengths. To Kladstrup it was liberal simple—give the criminals what they want, watches and money that can be replaced, and they *might* leave without the loss of human lives that can't be replaced. To Thomas things were also simple, but more realistically so.

By pointing guns at him and demanding his watches and money, those criminals indicated that they were willing to take his life if he didn't cooperate with them. Other shopkeepers who had apparently cooperated with robbers had been killed. He was at the mercy of criminals. Whether he lived or died was up to *them*. A tug on the trigger by any of those thugs, and he was history. The only way that he could take that decision away from them and ensure his survival was to get the thugs before they could, possibly on the basis of no more than a whim, shoot him. Simple! But Kladstrup, the reporter, showed no sign of ever getting it, and neither did anyone else associated with *Turning Point*.

As mainstream-media treatments of anything pertaining to guns go, *Turning Point's* examination of the use of guns for self-defense was far from the worst. Thomas was allowed to tell his story and self-defense instructor and firearms authority Massad Ayoob and several of his students were interviewed and shown going through their firearms training. But the impression couldn't be left that ABC was endorsing the notion that common citizens should arm themselves for the purpose of self-defense. So after Thomas' story was told, *two* other stories were used to illustrate how carrying a gun for self-protection could cause problems. In one of these, a Marine home on leave shot and wounded a person who was running away from him after trying to steal his car at a car wash. Though the thief was running away and seemed to pose no threat to the Marine, a grand jury, apparently fed up with criminals, refused to indict the Marine for shooting him. In the other case, a middle-aged motorist shot and killed a teenager who had punched him after being called to task for reckless driving.

And *Gunfighter Nation* author Richard Slotkin was called upon to make some solemn and politically-correct comments about the continuing American attachment to guns that he obviously considered to be retrograde. In response to Thomas' expression of concern that his fellow shopkeepers had come to view him as a hero, and might feel that they could arm themselves and follow his lead without preparing themselves as he had for such armed confrontations, Slotkin commented: "If you see Lance Thomas as a hero, then you're not really listening to what Lance Thomas is telling you about his life, because to resist force with force converts a situation of possible deadly threat into one in which firing back is more or less inevitable. It doesn't make you more invulnerable to such violence, in a way it makes you more vulnerable." Slotkin apparently thinks that heroism is risk-free.

Thomas, who could easily have been killed by any of the six robbers who had been pointing guns at him when he shot them, apparently had, in ways understandable only in the enlightened circles inhabited by the likes of Slotkin and reporter Kladstrup, acted unreasonably. Yes, as Thomas acknowledged, even though he had survived them and strongly felt that he had acted justifiably in each case, and he in no way regretted them, those defense shootings changed his life. Concerned about his own safety, he gave up his business and took steps to evade gang thugs looking for revenge. But what was his alternative to meeting force with force? Cooperate with the robbers and *hope* that they wouldn't kill him (and some of his customers) as they had killed other shopkeepers? Cooperate with them and *hope* that they wouldn't show their appreciation by returning over and over again until they finally killed someone and/or ruined his business? If good people like Thomas (and the citizens of old Northfield and Coffeyville) aren't willing to put their lives on the line to combat thugs, who will? The police, who weren't there, and couldn't reasonably be expected to be there, when he and his fellow shopkeepers needed them?

However, such concerns wouldn't phase Slotkin, Kladstrup, and other modern enlightened "consumers of safety," as attorney and Second Amendment defender Jeffrey Snyder might label them. Writing after 1999's Colorado school massacre of 12 students and a teacher by a pair of demented students, and after the citizens of Missouri had voted down the right to carry concealed handguns for self-protection, Snyder noted: "The reason why laws selling crime prevention have such tremendous appeal is that most Americans conceive themselves as mere passive consumers of a product called 'safety,' created for and delivered to them by government." And, he continued, "Inhabiting a world in which everyone believes that having the desire and the wherewithal to confront murderers in the act of murder is beyond their ability, and someone else's responsibility, they call 911, fall in abject terror, or wait and cower, passive recipients of a service that they hope will be delivered in timely fashion." Snyder knows that we're not all safety consumers. Florida State criminologist Gary Kleck estimates defensive gun use in the United States at more than 2.5 million times per year (in most cases the gun wasn't fired), and other studies place that number between 760,000 and 3.6 million.

And it should be noted that several mass shootings have been stopped by armed or unarmed private citizens acting in the spirit of Northfield and Coffeyville before the police arrived. The Pearl, Mississippi school shooting was stopped by an assistant principal armed with a pistol that he retrieved from his car which, because it had a gun in it, had to be parked far off campus. That principal was a member of an organization much endowed with the spirit of Northfield and Coffeyville, the National Rifle Association (NRA), and consequently, much reviled in enlightened safety-consuming circles.

The Edinboro, Pennsylvania school shooting was halted by the shotgun-armed owner of the banquet hall where an eighth-grade graduation dance was being held and where the shooting took place. An unarmed, wounded student, also an NRA member, stopped the Springfield, Oregon shooting by wrestling the shooter to the floor. Unarmed fellow passengers grabbed the Long Island Railroad shooter when he was trying to reload. Had any of those passengers been armed, they could have stopped him sooner.

But surely the most spectacular example of ordinary people thwarting a mass shooting and exhibiting the spirit of Northfield and Coffeyville in spades occurred far from the United States. Back in 1984, when three terrorists entered a Jerusalem café bent on machine-gunning as many people as possible before moving on to other crowded places to massacre more innocents before the police or army could stop them, they managed to kill only one person before being shot down by pistol-packing Israeli civilians. The single survivor told the press the next day that he and his partners had not known that Israeli civilians packed heat. How ironic! The Israeli government even encourages civilians to carry guns for the protection of themselves and their communities, while in the United States most of the prominent Jews in politics and the media encourage the consumption of safety, and most of the Jewish community seems dedicated to such consumption.

In 1990, a gentleman claiming to be a Jewish survivor of Treblinka, the Nazi death camp, wrote to a gun magazine in the hope that he could convince even one gun owner to turn in his guns. Concerned about the "gun violence" he saw everywhere in New York, he associated it with the guns carried by the Nazis who came to take him to the camp. Never mind that thugs use guns to cause problems in this country and government agents used them to commit atrocities in Nazi Germany, he was shocked to learn "that the United States says that Americans actually have the right to own guns."

If not for the fact that so many American Jews, from the Diane Feinsteins and Charles Schumers in government, to the Richard Cohens in journalism, to the Barbara Streisands in entertainment, to the anonymous man and woman on the street regularly express similar sentiments, it would be difficult to take that letter seriously. How could a people who have so often been horribly victimized by the armed agents of governments in various parts of the world trust the armed agents of government in this country to keep them safe?

The same question could be asked of blacks, prominent and otherwise, who support civilian disarmament in this country and look to the police for protection. As late as the civil rights movement of the 1960s, Ku Klux Klan meetings were advertised and members of that organization recruited at the police stations of some Southern towns.

But the spirit of Northfield and Coffeyville lives in some American Jews, as indicated by the letter responses by two Jews to the letter of the anti-gun Holocaust survivor. The first, from the founder of Jews for the Preservation of Firearms Ownership, stated: "There has not been, and I predict never will be, a time when people will be better off by being disarmed and naively allowing the government of any nation the power to determine who will be free." The second, from the son of a Holocaust survivor, stated that his father had determined that "never again would he or his family be rounded up like sheep for the slaughter! They would have the will, the training, and the means to fight back. He taught us that to die fighting tyranny like this is preferable to what happened to our friends and relatives under Nazis." Here is recognition, shared by the Founders of our country, that threats to the survival of decent people can come not only from criminals but from their own government.

When you get right down to it, the spirit of Northfield and Coffeyville is the spirit of self-governing people and of the Constitution and the Bill of Rights. The Founders didn't expect us to consume safety; they expected us to be directly involved in the ongoing defense of ourselves, our families, our communities, our country, and our way of life. When the citizens of Missouri, the home state of the James-Younger gang, had the chance to determine by vote whether or not they would be allowed, like the citizens of 31 other states, to obtain permits to carry handguns concealed for defensive purposes, the urban counties containing St. Louis and Kansas City were responsible for the narrow defeat of that measure. No surprise. Unfortunately, as we move into the 21st century, American urban and suburban areas are producing far more safety consumers than they are people like Lance Thomas.

RACISM, ELITISM, AND GUN CONTROL

Original manuscript of an essay first published as "Gun Control: White Man's Law" in Reason, *December, 1985, and reprinted in one form or another in* The Washington Times, Cleveland Plain Dealer, Baltimore Sun, Monitor (the journal of the National Rifle Association's Institute for Legislative Action), *1985,* Second Amendment Foundation's Monograph Series, *1986,* The Informed Argument: A Multidisciplinary Reader and Guide, *1986 1ˢᵗ edition through 1998 5ᵗʰ edition, and* The Reason Gun Reader, *1993.*

Chances are very good that the reader has never heard of General Laney. He hasn't had a brilliant military career that I know of. In fact, I'm not certain that he has even served in the military. General, you see, isn't Laney's rank. General is Laney's first name. General Laney, however, has a certain claim to fame—a claim that has yet to be widely recognized. He is a politically-involved black man who lives in Detroit, but his political involvement isn't of the sort that can be expected to draw major media attention at the national level. Laney isn't following in the pacifistic footsteps of Martin Luther King, Jr., and he has little in common with Jesse Jackson or with the militant blacks of the 1960s and '70s.

General Laney is the founder of, and the moving force behind, a little-publicized organization known as the National Black Sportsman's Association, an organization also known as the Black Gun Lobby. And Laney has been quoted as follows: "Gun control is really race control. People who embrace gun control are really racists in nature. All gun laws have been enacted to control certain classes of people, mainly black people, but the same laws used to control blacks are being used to disarm white people as well."

After reading the preceding quotation, I suspect that even most liberals and neo-liberals, blacks as well as whites, will be inclined to assign to General Laney a black extremist label, but the assignment of such a label might be a little premature in Laney's case. After all, some white liberals have said essentially the same thing about gun controls that Laney has said. In his book, *Saturday Night Special,* investigative reporter Robert Sherrill, himself no lover of guns, concluded that the object of the Gun Control Act of 1968 was black control rather than gun control. According to Sherrill, Congress was so panicked by the ghetto riots of 1967 and 1968 that the aim of GCA 1968 was to "shut off weapons access to blacks, and since they [Congress] probably associated cheap guns with ghetto blacks and thought cheapness was peculiarly the characteristic of imported military surplus and the mail-order traffic, they decided to cut off these sources while leaving over-the-counter purchases open to the affluent." While the Congressional motivation behind GCA 1968 may have been more complex than Sherrill suggests, keeping blacks from acquiring guns certainly may have been part of that motivation, even though Congress seems to have been totally wrong concerning the actual sources of black armament.

There seems to be little doubt, however, that the earliest "Saturday night special" controls in the United States were blatantly racist and elitist in their intent. As San Francisco civil liberties attorney Don B. Kates, Jr., an opponent of gun prohibitions, but one with impressive liberal credentials (he has been a law clerk for William Kunstler, a civil rights activist in the South, and an Office of Economic Opportunity lawyer), has made clear in his book *Restricting Handguns: The Liberal Skeptics Speak Out,* prohibitions against the sale of cheap handguns originated in the post-Civil War South. Small revolvers selling for as little as 50 or 60 cents became available in the 1870s and 1880s. Since they could be afforded by recently-emancipated blacks and poor whites (whom agrarian agitators of the time were encouraging to ally for economic and political purposes), these guns constituted a significant threat to a Southern establishment interested in maintaining pre-war social stratification patterns in the post-war era. Consequently, as Kates notes, in 1870 Tennessee banned "selling all but 'the Army and Navy model' handgun, i.e., the most expensive one, which was beyond the means of most blacks and laboring people." In 1881, Arkansas enacted an almost identical ban on the sale of cheap revolvers, while in 1902, South Carolina banned the sale of all handguns to all but "sheriffs and their special deputies—i.e., company goons and the KKK," and in 1893 and 1907, respectively, Alabama and Texas attempted to put handguns out of the reach of blacks and poor whites through "extremely heavy business and/or transactional taxes" on the sale of such weapons. Pre-emancipation bans on arms possession by blacks continued to be enforced by hook or by crook in those Deep South states that didn't see fit to enact new gun laws.

The cheap revolvers of the late 19th and early 20th centuries came to be referred to as "Suicide Specials," the "Saturday night special" label not being generally attached to such weapons until reformers and politicians again became concerned about them during the 1960s. And the source of this more recent concern about cheap revolvers, as their newer label seems to indicate, has much in common with the concerns manifested by gun law initiators of the post-Civil War South. As B. Bruce-Briggs has written in his *Public Interest* article, "The Great American Gun War," "It is difficult to escape the conclusion that the 'Saturday Night Special' is emphasized because it is cheap and is being sold to a particular class of people. The name is sufficient evidence—the reference is to 'nigger-town Saturday night.'" For those who argue that the concern about cheap handguns is justified because these guns are used in most gun crimes, it should be noted that not even the anti-gun author of *Saturday Night Special,* Robert Sherrill, takes this position, and James D. Wright, Peter H. Rossi, and Kathleen Daly, the sociologist authors of *Under the Gun: Weapons, Crime, and Violence in America,* which is based on an exhaustive, federally-funded, critical review of gun-issue research, have found no conclusive proof that cheap handguns are used in crime more often than are expensive handguns. Of course, the makers of quality arms, looking out for their own interests, have sometimes supported bans on cheap handguns and bans on the importation of cheap military surplus weapons, but it is difficult to avoid the conclusion that cheap handguns are threatening primarily because troublesome minorities and the potentially troublesome poor can afford them.

Attempts to regulate the possession of firearms began in the northern states during the early part of the 20th century, and although these regulations had a different focus than those that had been concocted in the South, they were no less racist and/or elitist in effect or intent than were the southern laws. Rather than in one way or another trying to keep handguns out of the price range that blacks and the poor in general could afford, New York's trend-setting Sullivan Law, enacted in 1911, simply required a police permit for legal possession of a handgun. This law made it possible for the police to screen applicants for permits to possess handguns, and while such a requirement may seem reasonable, it can be and has been abused easily. Members of groups not in favor with the political establishment or the police are automatically suspect, and find it to be almost impossible to obtain a permit, and when the Sullivan Law was enacted, Southern and Eastern European immigrants were suspect. Most of these immigrants were considered to be racially distinct and inferior, and they were also religiously or ideologically suspect due either to their Catholicism or Judaism, or to the anarchism or radicalism associated with their groups. Consequently, the actual radical political activities or criminal activities of some of these people only reinforced the stereotypes associated with all of them to the point that Southern and Eastern European immigrants in general couldn't be trusted with guns. Over the years, application of the Sullivan Law has become increasingly elitist as the police have become reluctant to grant handgun permits to any but the wealthy or the politically influential. This elitism is beautifully exemplified by the fact that while the *New York Times* often editorializes against the private possession of handguns, the publisher of that newspaper, A. O. Sulzberger, has admitted that he possesses a hard-to-get permit not only to own but to carry a handgun. His admission came after the *New York Daily News* and the *Wall Street Journal* found out about his permit. Another such permit was possessed by the husband of Dr. Joyce Brothers, the pop psychologist who has claimed that firearms ownership is indicative of male sexual inadequacy or dysfunction.

It isn't my intention to provide a detailed history of the attempts that have been made to regulate the private possession of firearms in the United States, but the preceding examples of such efforts should be enough to suggest that far from being simple crime-control measures, gun controls have not-very-well-hidden racist, or at least elitist agendas of the sort attributed to them by General Laney. And efforts to control guns have been bound up with such agendas for centuries, whenever and wherever such efforts have been made. Even though European aristocrats were members of a weapons-loving warrior caste, they did their best to keep the gun from becoming a weapon of war. It was certainly all right to kill with civilized weapons such as the sword, the battle ax, or the lance, weapons that the armored knights were trained to use and which gave them a tremendous advantage over commoners who didn't have the training of the knights or possess their expensive weapons and armor. But as they became more effective weapons with the capability of piercing armor, guns democratized warfare and even made common soldiers more than a match for the armored and aristocratic knights, thereby threatening the very existence of the feudal aristocracy. A few centuries earlier, the Church had attempted to keep Christians from using another armor-piercing, knight-threatening projectile weapon, the crossbow, against each other in battle, though it was perfectly all right to use such weapons against pagans and infidels.

For various reasons, the European aristocracy wasn't able to control gun use, and at least in part, gun use helped to bring down that aristocracy and feudalism. The story was different in Japan, however, where during the 17th century the Tokugawa Shogunate, due to various political, cultural, and geographical factors, was able to establish a rigidly stratified society that de-emphasized the development of guns and restricted arms possession to a warrior aristocracy, the samurai. When Commodore Perry "reopened" Japan to the rest of the world in the middle of the 19th century, few Japanese were familiar with guns (the sword was the most honored weapon of the samurai), and the guns with which some were familiar were matchlocks only somewhat improved over those introduced to Japan by the Portuguese toward the middle of the 16th century. As post-Perry Japan modernized and acquired a modern military, it also quickly developed modern weaponry. But a citizenry with no gun-owning tradition was easily kept in place and gunless in an extremely collectivist-oriented society where individuals were more susceptible to informal and formal social controls than westerners are likely to be aware of or to appreciate.

As early as 1541, England enacted a law that limited legal possession of handguns and crossbows (weapons considered to be criminally troublesome) to those with incomes *exceeding 100 pounds a year*, though long gun possession wasn't restricted—*except for Catholics,* a potentially troublesome minority after the English Reformation. Catholics couldn't legally keep militia-type weapons in their homes, as other Englishmen were encouraged to do, but they could legally possess defensive weapons—except, as Bill of Rights authority Joyce Lee Malcolm has noted, during times "of extreme religious tension." With the restoration of Charles II in 1660, an attempt to disarm a heavily armed English populace was made with the purpose of keeping that populace from causing problems for the new king. According to Malcolm, when William and Mary came to the English throne, they were presented with a list of rights, one of which was aimed at staving off any future attempt at arms confiscation—"all Protestant citizens had a right to keep arms for their defence." England then remained free of very restrictive gun legislation until 1920, when even though the crime rate was *very low,* concern about radicals and others who were *politically troublesome* ushered in today's very restrictive gun laws. Interestingly enough, as Colin Greenwood, once Superintendent of the West Yorkshire Metropolitan Police, discovered through his research at Cambridge University, the English gun crime rate is significantly higher now than it was before that nation's strict gun laws were enacted.

Again, the preceding are just examples of the political uses to which gun controls have been put in other parts of the world, and Nazi Germany, the Soviet Union, and South Africa need only be mentioned to suggest the extremes to which these social-control measures have been carried in modern times. Raymond G. Kessler, a lawyer/sociologist who has provided some of the most sociologically-sophisticated insights into the gun control issue, suggests that attempts to regulate the civilian possession of firearms have no less than five political functions: they "(1) increase citizen reliance on government and tolerance of increased police powers and abuse; (2) help prevent opposition to government; (3) facilitate repressive action by government and its allies; (4) lessen the pressure for major or radical reform; and (5) can be selectively enforced against those perceived to be a threat to government."

Of course, while the more idealistic proponents of gun controls might acknowledge that such measures have been used in the ways that Kessler has mentioned, they would most certainly deny that the controls that they support are either racist or elitist in intent or effect, since they would apply to everybody and are aimed at reducing violence for everybody. Yet the controls that they advocate can hardly avoid being racist, or at least classist, in effect, and only the naive or the dishonest can claim that they aren't elitist in intent.

First, consider the almost certain racist or classist effects of, say, handgun prohibition. Kessler has also written that while liberals are likely to sympathize with the poor and minorities responsible for so much of this nation's violent crime, when victimized themselves, "or when they hear of an especially heinous crime, liberals, like most people, feel anger and hostility toward the offender. The discomfort of having incompatible feelings can be alleviated by transferring the anger away from the offender to an inanimate object—the weapon." A perfect example of this sort of transference is provided by Pete Shields, the chairman of Handgun Control Incorporated, whose son was killed with a handgun by one of San Francisco's Zebra killers—blacks who were killing whites at random as the opportunity presented itself. This tragic killing was carried out by a black man who was after whites. His own skin color and that of his victim were important to the killer. But in his grief, the white liberal father couldn't let the skin color of his son's killer make a difference—that would smack of white racism. So the gun was the culprit (even though some of the Zebra killings were carried out with knives), and we now have Handgun Control Incorporated with its focus on the "victims of handguns," but no mention of the victims of black racists. Yet blacks and minorities in general are likely to be adversely affected the most by legislation proposed by Handgun Control Incorporated and other proponents of strict handgun controls such as the National Coalition to Ban Handguns.

Since the illegal possession of a handgun (or of any gun) is a crime that in itself doesn't produce a victim or a complainant likely to report that crime to the police, handgun permit requirements or outright handgun prohibitions aren't easily enforced. And as civil liberties attorney Kates has observed, when laws are difficult to enforce, "enforcement becomes progressively more haphazard until at last the laws are used only against those who are unpopular with the police"—back to Kessler's fifth political function of gun control concerning selective enforcement. Of course, minorities, especially minorities who don't "know their place," aren't likely to be popular with the police, and these very minorities, in the face not only of police indifference to their safety but of police antagonism toward them as well, may be the most inclined to look to guns for protection— guns that they can't acquire legally and that place them in jeopardy if possessed illegally. While the intent of such laws may not be racist or classist, therefore, their ironic effect can be racist or classist.

Regarding the elitist nature of the measures proposed by even the most idealistic proponents of gun controls, several students of the ongoing battle over gun controls see that battle as being between what a *Wall Street Journal* article once referred to as "cosmopolitan America" and "bedrock America." Briefly the argument goes as follows: Though there are exceptions to the rule, the most dedicated and vociferous proponents of the strictest gun controls are urban or urban-oriented, upper-middle class or aspiring upper-middle class, change-oriented liberals or cosmopolitans, many of whom are part of what neo-conservatives view as a knowledge-producing and knowledge-disseminating New Class (establishment intellectuals and the media), and most of them know little or nothing about guns or the wide range of legitimate uses to which they (even handguns) are regularly put, but associate guns with war, crime, and the cruelties of the hunt. On the other hand, the most dedicated, though often inarticulate opponents of such measures seem to be rural- or small-town-oriented, working or middle class, tradition-oriented conservatives or bedrockers, few of whom possess the means to publicize their views, but many of whom know a great deal about guns and the wide range of legitimate uses to which they are regularly put and associate them with freedom, security, and wholesome recreation. Change-oriented cosmopolitans tend to believe in social engineering (school busing, affirmative action, etc.), but a heavily armed civil populace might make social engineering a risky business as the assassinations, riots, and other violent events of the last few decades may *seem* to have made clear. The battle over gun controls, therefore, has come about as hard-core cosmopolitan America has attempted to impose its anti-gun lifestyles and world views on a bedrock America that is comfortable with guns (including handguns), seldom misuses them (most gun crime is urban), and sees them as protection against criminal victimization and/or government oppression. To the extent that this imposition can be accomplished, anti-gun cosmopolitan America loses nothing and gains peace of mind while attempting to bring about social change through social engineering, social change that as a whole bedrock America is likely to approve of no more than it approves of the loss of its guns and the way of life associated with them—progress in the eyes of the elite cosmopolitans, but 1984 or brave new world in the eyes of the increasingly subjugated bedrockers.

How right you are, General Laney—"All gun laws have been enacted to control certain classes of people...."

GUN CONTROL AND ELITES OF THE RIGHT AND LEFT

Originally published as "Guns and the Ruling Elite" in Liberty, *September, 1996, and reprinted as "Gun Control and Elites of the Right and Left" in* Gun News Digest, *Winter, 1996.*

"The right of citizens to bear arms is just one more guarantee against arbitrary government, one more safeguard against a tyranny which now appears remote in America, but which historically has proved to be always possible." For several decades now, and particularly since the tragic terrorist bombing of the federal offices in Oklahoma City, cosmopolitan politicians such as Congressman Charles Schumer (D-New York) and most establishment journalists have dismissed statements such as this as dangerous right-wing rhetoric. But these are not the words of a right-wing reactionary. They are the words of a liberal's liberal, Hubert H. Humphrey, who had a far better grasp of the concerns of the Founding Fathers than does the Yale law-school graduate currently occupying the White House.

Since the dawn of history when agriculture and its food surpluses made elites possible, they have, with varying degrees of success, attempted to reserve arms-bearing privileges for themselves in order that they could better control the non-elite rest of us. Though our Founding Fathers were hardly devoid of vested interests of their own, those vested interests fostered in them such a distrust of government, standing armies, and even militia of the selective rather than the all-encompassing variety, that they supported widespread arms possession on the part of the citizenry through the Second

Amendment to the Constitution of the United States: "A well regulated Militia being necessary to the security of a Free State, the right of the people to keep and bear Arms, shall not be infringed."

That the militia to which this amendment refers was grounded in a populace exercising what was believed to be its "natural right" to arms and was composed of the entire male citizenry of military age, not a National Guard-type "select militia," is beyond reasonable dispute. This reading of the amendment has been supported not only through the works of such prominent, liberal, non-gun-owning Second Amendment scholars as Akhil R. Amar of Yale, William Van Alstyne of Duke, and Sanford Levinson of the University of Texas, but by the Founders themselves. According to Richard Henry Lee, "A militia, when properly formed, are in fact the People themselves . . . and include all men capable of bearing arms." And George Mason agreed: "Who are the militia? They consist now of the whole people, except a few public officers." Those who would argue that such a people's militia is outdated receive no support from current Federal regulations pertaining to the composition of the militia—practically all able-bodied males and some females between the ages of 17 and 45 who are citizens of the United States or have declared an intention to become citizens. The National Guard is still only the organized and federalizeable part of the militia.

And the Founders intended citizens to possess arms not only to protect themselves and others from criminals and their nation from other nations, but to rebel against their own government if it became too oppressive. Tench Coxe, a friend of James Madison, wrote: "As civil rulers, not having their duty to the people before them, may attempt to tyrannize, and as the military forces which must be occasionally raised to defend our country, might pervert their power to the injury of their fellow-citizens, the people are confirmed by the next article in their right to keep and bear their private arms."

It is this protection-against-tyranny aspect of *private* weapons possession that elite gun prohibitionists once conveniently overlooked, but since Oklahoma City vehemently reject. Humphrey did not overlook or reject this concern and neither has prominent liberal legal scholar Levinson, who, referring to the treatment of Chinese students at Tianannen Square and modern guerrilla warfare, has written: "The fact that these may not be pleasant examples does not affect the principal point, that a state facing a totally disarmed population is in a far better position, for good or ill, to suppress popular demonstrations and uprisings than one that must calculate the possibilities of its soldiers and officials being injured or killed." However, modern elites of the right as well as the left have vested interests in regulating civilian access to guns.

Traditional Business Elite Vested Interests

With the industrialization of the United States, the ascendant captains of industry were less interested in encouraging the development of an independent armed yeomanry capable of standing up to its own government than they were in encouraging the development of a compliant work force. Of course, urbanization and immigration accompanied industrialization, and the mix did not produce the stability desired by the business elites. As social historian Altina Waller has noted, local progressive elites had seen the Hatfield-McCoy feud as standing in the way of "economic and social 'progress.' Once feuding, whiskey, and guns were eliminated, these people argued, an impartial judicial system would readily bring about order. Now coal companies enforced their wishes with guns, reinforced by a county government and judicial system they had bought and paid for."

According to John Ellis, during the late 19th and the pre-World War I 20th centuries when the traditional military establishments of industrial Europe and the United States ignored machine guns, European colonizers (civilian as well as military) were using them to subjugate poorly-armed natives (particularly in Africa), while American National Guardsmen and company guards were using them "as an alternative to collective bargaining" against organizing labor. In 1896, for example, Chicago Commercial Club members contributed $2,000 (over $32,000 in today's money) within 48 hours to buy a machine gun for the Illinois National Guard for possible use against labor rioters. The notorious Baldwin-Felts Detective Agency transferred at least eight machine guns from West Virginia to Colorado to keep striking miners under control during the troubles of 1912-1913. During this period, the companies regularly used machine-gun-equipped trains to patrol and strafe the Cabin Creek and Paint Creek areas, and at Ludlow in 1914, National Guardsmen machine gunned the miner's tent colony. Bullets and the fire that resulted claimed 36 lives and injured over 100 others. Needless to say, such uses of the machine gun by the authorities and business elites produced no government reaction against these weapons.

Of course, traditional or conservative elite efforts to maintain control have seldom been subtle. Weapons are acceptable in the right hands—theirs and those of their hired enforcers. The National Firearms Act of 1934 partially subverted the protection-against-tyranny purpose of private arms possession supported by the Founders by bringing the *legal* civilian possession of small arms of obvious military value, such as full-automatics and sawed-off rifles and shotguns, under the direct control of the very government that the citizenry might feel obliged to resist. This regulation of the civilian possession of such arms was allegedly needed because they were what would now be called the "weapons of choice" of the gangsters and bank robbers of the 1920s and 1930s—handguns having almost been included in this regulated category. However, such notorious characters of the day as John Dillinger and Bonnie and Clyde got their automatic weapons by stealing them from the police and National Guard, or by having underworld gunsmiths convert one-shot-per-trigger-pull semiautomatics to automatics that keep firing as long as the trigger is held back. And the only thing accomplished by the $200 transfer tax (over $2,000 in today's money) a legal purchaser of these regulated items must pay to the federal government was to put such guns out of the financial reach of most people who could pass the background check. While inflation has lowered this tax barrier considerably for more recent purchasers, in 1934 only the wealthy could afford the tax and regulated arms at a time when Depression-spawned mass demonstrations such as the march on the Ford plant in Dearborn, Michigan and the World War I veterans' march on Washington, D.C. had the establishment worried about a rebellion. In other words, as gun-control opponent Neal Knox has noted, lawmakers may have had disgruntled citizens rather than submachine-gun-armed bank robbers in mind when they passed the 1934 Act.

To be sure, business elite efforts to keep workers unarmed and docile have not always received local, state, or federal government support as the United States has industrialized. In 1921, for example, the North Carolina Supreme Court acknowledged the need that the poor and the unpopular might have for guns: "This is not an idle or an obsolete guarantee, for there are still localities, not necessary to mention, where great corporations, under the guise of detective agents or police forces, terrorize their employees by armed force. If the people are forbidden to carry the only arms within their means, among them pistols, they will be completely at the mercy of these plutocratic organizations."

And at times during the 20th century, establishment military needs and our libertarian militia tradition have coincided in such a fashion that ordinary citizens have not only been encouraged to familiarize themselves with military small arms, but have been supplied with them at bargain prices by an agency of the federal government itself. The National Board for the Promotion of Rifle Practice was established in 1903 at a time when the United States was flexing its muscles internationally, and just after the Spanish-American War had demonstrated, as had the Civil War, that many recruits had brought no marksmanship skills into the military with them. The Army's Office of the Director of Civilian Marksmanship (DCM) was established in 1916 under the National Board as part of the National Defense Act that, among other things, paved the way for conscription as American involvement in World War I approached. After World War II and the beginning of the Cold War, it was the DCM that put hundreds of thousands of military small arms, including semiautomatic rifles, carbines, and pistols, and ammunition for them into civilian circulation. Ironically, therefore, for much of this century business-elite domestic interests in restricting civilian access to firearms have been offset by the international interests of the establishment in encouraging young men to acquire militarily-useful marksmanship skills. And while government efforts to arm civilians and teach them to shoot surely have not been motivated by protection-against-domestic-tyranny concerns (apart from the possible need to overthrow a domestic communist regime), these measures have been supportive of this traditional concern as well as of establishment foreign-intervention concerns of which the Founders would probably have disapproved. But things have changed dramatically over the past 30 years, as a new elite, though a fragmented one, has increasingly made its mark on the national scene as it has simultaneously supported and challenged the business elite.

Modern Knowledge Elite Vested Interests

The modern or liberal knowledge elite, the so called "New Class," is composed of professional thinkers and other word workers who create and transmit what passes for knowledge in our modern world, and certain varieties of these "experts" are inclined to take themselves, their offerings, and their interests quite seriously. As the gods once allegedly spoke to us through priests, now nature allegedly speaks to us through secular intellectuals (including secularized "social gospel" theologians) who are no less willing than the traditional priests to control our lives if given the chance, basing their authority on "science" rather than on supernatural connections. Such secular priests have been with us for quite some time. During the early 19th century, Frenchman Auguste Comte, generally credited with being the founder of sociology, envisioned a sociological secular priesthood that through its ongoing research efforts would scientifically determine the basis for social policy decisions. As sociologist Lewis Coser has summarized Comte's views on governance: "Only those willing to submit themselves to the rigorous constraints of scientific methodology and to the canons of scientific evidence can presume to have a say in the guidance of human affairs." Though such a priesthood has yet to be established, much of today's sociology is devoted to producing "knowledge" useful to social engineers.

Karl Marx turned social criticism into a "science," Sigmund Freud gave us a "scientific" secular confessional, and B. F. Skinner offered himself as a guide to Utopia through a "scientific" secular religion—stimulus-response behavioral psychology. And as psychiatrist and psychiatric critic Jonas Robitscher has noted: "The ultimate claim for psychiatry was that psychiatrists should screen and select world leaders, because social policy was too important to be left to unstable individuals who could not earn a psychiatric stamp of approval." But in his 1971 presidential address to the American psychological Association, Kenneth Clark advocated going beyond screening to developing aggression-reducing pills and force-feeding them to the world's leaders. This drug would subordinate man's "animalistic, barbaric and primitive propensities . . . to the uniquely human moral and ethical characteristics of love, kindness, empathy." And Frederick W. Taylor, the turn-of-the-century founder of "scientific management," and his followers were interested in extending their technocratic approach to organization far beyond business and industry to society as a whole. As Donald Stabile has convincingly argued, American socialism has long been permeated by a labor-alienating technocratic

Taylorism that undermines participatory planning and democracy.

A diverse collection of specialists subscribing to perspectives often very much at odds with each other, the influence of these various "experts" exists only to the extent that they can use the appearance of scientific objectivity and/ or detached rationality to cover their own vested interests and convince non-experts that "experts" know what they are talking about. But the people-manipulating interests of big business and industry and centralized big government, assisted by big education and big media, have left non-experts in these areas easy to convince. These interests have afforded various applied social and behavioral scientists, educators, specialists in communications, medicine, and management, and others claiming expertise in people-manipulation, coordination, processing, and so forth, the chance to entrench themselves in influential settings where they can encourage the "educated" classes to accept what economist and syndicated columnist Thomas Sowell has referred to as their "unconstrained vision" of man. According to Sowell, who does not subscribe to this vision himself, "Given that explicitly articulated knowledge is special and concentrated in the unconstrained vision, the best conduct of social activities depends upon the special knowledge of the few being used to guide the actions of the many." Sowell goes on to note, "It is consistent for the unconstrained vision to promote equalitarian ends by unequalitarian means, given the great differences between those whom [John Stuart] Mill called 'the wisest and best' and those who have not yet reached that intellectual and moral level." And sociologist Peter Berger, another scholarly critic of knowledge-elite pretensions, has called attention to this elite's vested interest in government intervention due to its heavy reliance on public sector employment. According to Berger, "Because government interventions have to be legitimated in terms of social ills, the New Class has a vested interest in portraying American society as a whole, and specific aspects of that society in negative terms."

Through countless magazine and journal articles, newspaper stories, columns, and editorials, TV commentaries, documentaries, talk shows, situation comedies, and crime shows, and textbook treatments of the issue, America's knowledge-creating and -transmitting elites have, with relatively few exceptions, made it abundantly clear that they agree with sociologist Morris Janowitz: "I see no reason . . . why anyone in a democracy should own a weapon." Democracy, from this elite point of view, is something that "experts" know how to run better than do ordinary citizens, but these "experts" apparently recognize that while the pen may be mightier than the sword in the long run of history, the swordsman can make quick work of the penman in the short run of individual existence. If not sold on reforms deemed necessary by the all-knowing "experts," an armed populace might be troublesome. Therefore, the people-control-through-gun-control efforts of the knowledge elites not only converge with but transcend those of the traditional business elites. The business elites need only docile workers and consumers, while the knowledge elites need docile citizens who can be manipulated through elite-formulated state interventions—such as busing, affirmative action, quotas, and so forth, often assisted by an activist judiciary—intended either to homogenize the populace in order to abolish the conflict-generating differences within it, or to eliminate the conflict-generating aspects of these differences.

United States involvement in World War II and the Korean War halted the drive for gun controls that had peaked in the late 1930s, but by the late l950s efforts to regulate civilian gun ownership were reviving and the political assassinations, ghetto riots, and black and radical militancy of the 1960s gave them impetus. The first notable achievement of this effort was the Gun Control Act of 1968, which even anti-gun investigative reporter Robert Sherrill believes was an attempt to keep cheap military-surplus weapons out of the hands of militant blacks. And social analyst B. Bruce Briggs has claimed that efforts to ban cheap handguns, "Saturday night specials," may have been similarly motivated. After all, according to Bruce-Briggs, their very label was derived from "nigger-town Saturday night." And even though the ghettoes were relatively quiet for some time before the 1992 Los Angeles riots, it is hardly far-fetched to consider the possibility that both business- and knowledge-elite pressures to regulate semiautomatic paramilitary weapons have been motivated more by their potential use by minority and other militants than by their actual use by drug gangs. After all, while such weapons have been used in a small number of mass shootings perpetrated by emotionally-disturbed individuals, no systematic study of guns used in crimes, even in drug-war states like Florida and California, has yet supported the claims of the gun controllers that "semiautomatic assault weapons" are the "weapons of choice" of the drug gangs.

Even more suggestively, the sale of new full-automatics was federally banned in 1986, despite the fact that at the time not a single documented case existed of a *legally-owned* machine gun having been used in a homicide during the 52 years of federal control of their legal possession. And elite concerns about the potential use of semiautomatic and/or full-automatic firearms by militants, particularly by right-wing militants, was not always disguised by drug-war rhetoric even before the Oklahoma City bombing. A 1985 *Newsweek* cover story titled "Machine Gun USA" stated, "In fact, the exotic-weapons craze is nowhere more frightening than among fanatics of the far right—a loosely knit underground of racist, anti-Semitic, pseudo-Christian xenophobes with links to both the Ku Klux Klan and the American Nazis movement." This same theme appeared in "Assault Weapons and Accessories in America," a 1988 "report" written by gun-control guru Josh Sugarmann for the Education Fund to End Handgun Violence and (significantly) New Right Watch, and in Handgun Control Inc. anti-assault-weapon ads, but it now permeates the Oklahoma City-induced anti-militia tirades spouted by the mainstream media and cosmopolitan politicians.

In this age of specialists, violence has again become a job for experts, the professionals of the military and police forces, with the upper-middle-class symbol-manipulating knowledge elitists who are not very good at violence and disapprove of it only too glad to let others specialize in state-approved violence to preserve or impose a properly engineered and approved social order. Thus, the very standing military forces (plus the select militia) that the Founders considered to be the foremost threats to representative government and liberty, are accepted in enlightened circles as logical extensions of the division of professional labor.

Are the Founder's concerns outdated? When Lieutenant Commander Guy Cunningham, a Navy officer working on a master's thesis, asked 300 Marines via questionnaire if they "would fire upon U.S. citizens who refuse or resist confiscation of firearms banned by the U.S. government,"

61.66% indicated that they would not fire. That left 26.34% indicating that they would fire, and 12% expressing no opinion. Hardly reassuring!

Where once the people were trusted with arms to keep the government in line, now only the government can be trusted with arms to keep the people in line. And elitists, both traditional and modern, ignoring peaceful Switzerland where the government issues practically every male between 20 and 50 a true assault rifle capable of full-automatic fire to keep in his home, point to the rest of Europe, where government-sponsored collective violence has slaughtered tens of millions since the turn of the century, as a model for us to emulate.

It is true, of course, that a risk associated with an armed populace is that occasionally an individual who is not part of the thug community may harm innocents with his/her weapons. However, the risk associated with an unarmed populace is that it can be enslaved or annihilated by a rogue government. As James Madison, the author of the Second Amendment, and its past and present supporters have recognized, throughout history the unarmed have been safe only as long as the armed (criminals *or government agents)* have allowed them to be safe. We might beware of politicians, bureaucrats, intellectuals, journalists, and others who encourage us to believe that this amendment is outdated or does no more than guarantee our select militia, the National Guard, the right to bear arms. Many of these same people did their best to obstruct or ignore investigations of governmental wrong doing at Ruby Ridge and Waco.

ASSAULT WEAPONS AGAIN?

Originally published as "All Guns to the People" in the October/September, 2003 issue of Liberty.

Imagine, if you will, what would have happened if last fall's sniper rampage in the D.C. area had occurred with Bill Clinton or Al Gore occupying the White House. Add a House and Senate controlled by the Democrats. To put it mildly, the mainstream-media-assisted drum beat for more draconian gun controls would have been loud and continuous, and they likely would have been enacted. As it was, even the push for keeping a fired slug and cartridge on record as a "fingerprint" for each new gun as a means (that won't work) of tracing guns used in crimes didn't get very far. Why?

The Bush Administration has thus far been far more supportive of the Second Amendment than any recent administration and gave the media nothing to run with. And after the gun issue played a significant role in the Republican takeover of both houses of Congress in 1994, and Al Gore's loss of states, such as his own Tennessee, that could have put him in the White House in 2000, many Democrat strategists see gun control as a losing proposition. And the 9-11 terrorist attack drove home the point to many people that the government can't necessarily be relied upon to protect them, and encouraged them not to support more restrictions on the acquisition of guns with which they could protect themselves.

But the gun issue is now back in the news because in September, 2004 the ban on "assault weapons" and large-capacity magazines passed in 1994 will sunset. That means that the bans will expire unless Congress takes action to extend them or make them permanent. And the usual suspects are already back pushing for this to happen—California Democrat Senator Dianne Feinstein, the Senate sponsor of the original ban, and New York Democrat Senator Charles Schumer, another sponsor of the ban when he was a member of the House. But they have apparently been joined by, of all people, President George W. Bush. Whether Bush, whose attorney general, John Ashcroft, has taken a strong pro-Second Amendment stand, actually supports the ban or is simply trying to keep the gun prohibitionists off of his back while he depends on the Republican Congress to keep the ban extension from getting to his desk, is not clear.

So here we go again! The same tired old arguments will be trotted out and uncritically passed on to the public by the mainstream media, entertainment as well as news, and they will all be grounded in the enlightened conventional wisdom on guns in establishment media, academic, and political circles. This enlightened conventional wisdom assumes (1) that sporting guns are less potent power- and firepower-wise than military firearms, and (2) that while civilians may have legitimate reasons for owning the former, they have none for owning the latter. It is wrong on both counts. For most of our history, American civilians have not only owned military small arms but sporting and/or defensive guns with more power and/or firepower than military guns, and they have done so with the unquestioned full blessing of the Second Amendment to the Constitution.

When Attorney General Ashcroft acknowledged that the Second Amendment guaranteed an individual right to bear arms, the mainstream press treated his position as a conservative one, when in fact, as David Kopel has noted, he was "simply returning to a position held by United States attorneys general before the administration of Lyndon Johnson." And the paper trail left by the Founders clearly indicates that the militia of the Second Amendment was grounded in a citizenry made up of individuals exercising what they considered to be their pre-constitutional, natural right to keep and bear arms. Richard Henry Lee wrote, "A militia, when properly formed, are in fact the people themselves, and include all men capable of bearing arms." And this from George Mason: "Who are the militia? They consist now of the whole people, except a few public officers." Patrick Henry believed that "the great object is that every man be armed. Everyone who is able might have a gun." The Militia Act of 1792 considered all free white males of military age to be militiamen, and required them to own militarily-useful firearms—a requirement not always met. And it should be noted that according to the *US. Code Title 10, section 311 (a),* all able-bodied males between the ages of 17 and 45 who are citizens or have declared that they intend to become citizens are still members of the militia. The United States Supreme Court acknowledged all of this about the militia of the Founders in *United States v Miller* (1939), and stated "that ordinarily when called for service these men were *expected to appear bearing arms supplied by themselves and of the kind in common use at the time"* (emphasis added).

And statements by prominent Americans from the founding generation to the recent past make it clear why such a militia has long been considered necessary. Tench Coxe, a friend of Bill of Rights author James Madison, wrote: "As civil rulers, not having their duty to the people before them, may attempt to tyrannize, and as the military forces which must be occasionally raised to defend our country, might pervert their power to the injury of their fellow citizens, the people are confirmed by the next article in their right to keep and bear their *private* arms" (emphasis added). Richard Henry Lee agreed: "To preserve liberty it is essential that the whole body of the people always possess arms and be taught alike, especially when young, how to use them. . . ." So did Noah Webster: "Before a standing army can rule, the people must be disarmed; as they are in almost every Kingdom of Europe. The supreme power in America cannot enforce unjust laws by the sword because the whole body of the people are armed." And Elbridge Gerry: "What, sir, is the use of militia? It is to prevent the establishment of a standing army, the bane of liberty." And Joseph Story, Associate Justice of the United States from 1811 to 1845: "The right of the citizens to keep and bear arms has justly been considered, as the palladium of the liberties of the republic; since it offers a strong moral check against usurpation and arbitrary power of the rulers; and will generally, even if these are successful in the first instance; enable the people to resist and triumph over them." Even the late Hubert H. Humphrey, the liberal Democrat senator and vice president, issued the following statement in 1959: "The right of citizens to bear arms is just one more guarantee against arbitrary government, one more safe-guard against tyranny which now appears remote in America, but which historically has proved to be always possible." And this from Judge Ronald M. Gould of the ultra-liberal US 9th Circuit Court of Appeals in his recent rebuff of a fellow judge's "December dicta remarks about the meaning of the Second Amendment:" "[T]he Second Amendment was designed by the Framers of our Constitution to safeguard our Nation not only in times of good government, such as we have enjoyed for generations, but also in the event, however unlikely, that our government or leaders would go bad. And it was designed to provide national security not only when our country is strong but also if it were to become weakened or otherwise subject to attack."

Judge Gould's recent comments concerning the purpose of the Second Amendment are very timely, because the liberal left, particularly since the Oklahoma City terrorist bombing and all the attention it brought to the militia movement, has demagogued against this "insurrectionist" interpretation of the amendment. How dare anyone suggest that American citizens would ever have to take up arms against their own government! And the American talk-radio right, particularly since the terrorism of 9-11, is so enamored of our military and police forces that it apparently can't conceive of them ever being used to establish a tyranny. But as Gould implies, the amendment's purpose is to provide a means for the citizenry to protect itself *when things have gone very wrong.* While our government is not now tyrannical, is it really less likely to become so at some future date than it was in the early days of the republic? And can today's large professional military be trusted with advanced firearms while civilians can't be trusted with them? What reason would we have to answer "yes" to either of these questions? The liberal establishment has long viewed the Constitution as an obstacle to its social engineering efforts, we now have exactly the kind of large professional military the Founders feared, and who knows what impact the war on terrorism will have on our civil liberties. In fact, with respect to the last point, even to voice such concerns since 9-11 is to risk earning the suspicion of the FBI's Joint Terrorism Task Force, which reportedly has been cautioning law enforcement to look out for "defenders of the U.S. Constitution against the federal government and the UN. . . ." That's scary!

Even when they acknowledge that the Founders did indeed intend that the citizenry be armed, opponents of widespread gun ownership in this country are quick to respond that what was acceptable and needed in the late 18th century is no longer acceptable or needed. The rapid-fire guns of today, they claim, are capable of doing far more damage than the single-shot muzzle-loading muskets, rifles, and pistols used by both soldiers and civilians at the time of the founding. Civilians can't be trusted with these advanced guns, but the armed agents of the government apparently can be trusted with them. There are two glaring problems with this argument. The first problem is that it ignores the already-discussed reason that the Founders desired that the citizenry be armed—as a check against the tyrannical tendencies of government and standing military forces.

The second problem with the preceding argument is that it's grounded in phenomenal ignorance of the types of guns to which American citizens have had easy access until recently. It's true that when the Second Amendment was inserted into the Bill of Rights, the guns available to both soldiers and civilians were (with the exceptions of a few multi-barreled guns and a few guns that loaded from the breech) muzzle-loading single-shots. But even then, the Pennsylvania/Kentucky rifles favored by civilian frontiersmen were far more accurate over far greater ranges than were the smoothbore muskets used by the military. Muskets, which could also be owned by civilians, were cheaper to make and faster to load than rifles, however, and better fitted the battle tactics of the day. Those tactics had opposing armies march up to each other, fire several volleys at each other at close range, and then charge each other with bayonets. Rifles, however, were quite useful to the guerrilla fighters, snipers, and skirmishers who avoided head-on confrontations with troops set up in battle formations.

But while the guns known to the Founders were slow-loading devices, between the late 1830s and 1900, all of the technologies making rapid fire possible had not only been invented but reasonably well perfected—revolvers, self-contained metallic cartridges, lever actions, pump actions, semiautomatics (one shot per trigger pull), and automatics/ machine guns (that fire as long as the trigger is held back). And civilians who desired them and could afford them had access to guns utilizing these various technologies from the time their production began.

According to Wayne van Zwoll, of the 22,000 powerful .44-caliber Dragoon model revolvers produced by Colt between 1847 and 1861, only 9,380 were purchased by the government. From the late 1860s to the early 1890s, when most American soldiers were issued cartridge-firing but single-shot rifles, civilians had access not only to similar rifles but to rapid-fire, lever-action rifles with magazine capacities up to, in the case of the rare Evans, a staggering 34 rounds, though most were in the middle teens. Army officers on the frontier often purchased these civilian "sporting' repeating rifles to carry on military campaigns. By the turn of the century, civilians could purchase several models of semiautomatic pistols manufactured by foreign and domestic companies, but our military didn't adopt a semiautomatic pistol until 1911. And our military didn't adopt a semiautomatic rifle until some 30 years after semiautomatic "sporting" rifles were introduced. Pump and semiautomatic shotguns used by the police for riot control and the military for trench and/or jungle warfare are adaptations of civilian sporting guns. The cartridges for which practically all of our military rifles, shotguns, and pistols have been chambered have also been favorites for hunting, target shooting, and/or self-defense, and none of them even approach the power of the most powerful cartridges available for hunting the largest and most dangerous game—elephants, cape buffalo, lions, tigers, and grizzly bears, etc.

After our major wars, from the Civil War through Korea, and after our military's adoption of new service firearms, surplus military small arms have been sold off to the public at bargain prices. In the late 1940s, 5-shot, bolt-action, .30-06 1917 Enfields, our main battle rifle during World War I, could be purchased through the Army's Office of the Director of Civilian Marksmanship (DCM) for under $10.00 each. As late as the middle 1960s, World War II semiautomatic .30-caliber carbines, equipped with 15-round magazines but capable of using the full-automatic M2 carbine's 30-round magazines, and semiautomatic .45-caliber pistols could be purchased from the DCM for about $20.00 each. And until passage of the Gun Control Act of 1968, surplus military rifles and pistols from around the world, even 20mm semiautomatic anti-tank rifles, as well as sporting guns of all types could over most of the country be purchased through the mail with no background checks or age restrictions.

Americans have long had easy and even government-encouraged access not only to modern military small arms, but to civilian guns with as much or more power and/or firepower than military firearms. In fact, until passage of the National Firearms Act (NFA) of 1934, the only things that restricted civilian access to machineguns were desire and cost. But it was the 1934 Act, the constitutionality of which is questionable since it restricts civilian access to guns with obvious militia utility, that would eventually lead to ordinary American infantrymen being issued guns with greater firepower than American civilians are allowed to possess without government restrictions. The NFA didn't ban the civilian possession of machine guns and other weapons (such as sawed-off rifles and shotguns) covered by the act. It did require owners of such guns to be cleared by local police chiefs or sheriffs after a background check, registration of the guns, payment of a $200 transfer tax to the federal government (a significant sum to everyone but the rich in 1934), and so forth.

When the NFA was passed, ordinary infantrymen carried 5-shot, bolt-action, .30-06 rifles (1903 Springfields), while officers and others carried 1911 .45-caliber semiautomatic pistols. The 1911 .45 was sold to civilians, who could also buy bolt-action rifles comparable to the military rifle as well as faster-firing lever-action, pump, and semiautomatic sporting rifles. Portable automatic weapons, like the Thompson submachine gun and the Browning Automatic Rifle (BAR) had been developed, but weren't used by the military in large numbers until WWII. Even in that war, most American infantrymen were still issued rifles, by then the 8-shot semiautomatic Ml Garand. So even with the federal restrictions placed on the civilian possession of fully-automatic firearms, weaponry allowed the citizenry and its militia was still comparable to that issued to most individual infantrymen until 1957.

In 1957, our military adopted the 7.62x51mm M14 rifle which has a 20-round magazine and can be fired selectively-- automatically (as a machine gun) as well as semiautomatic—

though the automatic feature was blocked on most M14s because recoil made them difficult to control when so fired. And another selective-fire rifle, the milder-recoiling 5.56x45mm M16, which also utilizes a 20-round magazine, was adopted by our services in 1963 and finally generally replaced the M14 in 1970. Many of the semiautomatic Ml rifles replaced in service by these selective-fire rifles have been sold to civilians by the DCM or otherwise, as has been common practice throughout our national history when our military has adopted new guns. But surplus Ml4s or M16s, once the latter rifle is replaced, won't be sold off to the public, because some M14s and all M16s can be fired not only semiautomatic but automatically, or in the case of later M16s, burst fire (three shots per trigger pull). Civilian acquisition of such guns, therefore, would be restricted not only by the 1934 NFA, but by 1986 federal legislation that put a halt to machine guns legally entering civilian circulation, and by bans on the ownership of machine guns that several states have enacted. And the soon-to-sunset 1994 legislation even banned the further civilian acquisition of those civilian semiautomatic-only variations of military firearms capable of full-automatic fire that have been oxymoronically labeled "assault weapons" (semiautomatics aren't assault anything), and of detachable box magazines capable of holding more than 10 rounds.

All of these restrictions, plus those on handgun ammunition that can penetrate body armor worn by the police (but in three decades has yet to do so to kill a cop), fly in the face of the Second Amendment and American tradition. All trust government over the citizenry. The paper trail they left makes clear that the Founders considered government to be a necessary evil, distrusted its armed agents, and saw an armed citizenry as a check against its tyrannical tendencies. During the 20th century alone, governments around the world have massacred at least 170,000,000 of their own people, not counting war casualties, and the actions of our federal police at Ruby Ridge, Idaho and Waco, Texas, though small-scale, indicate that such things can happen here. Yet not only ignoring the Second Amendment paper trail and our firearms tradition, but denying their existence, the gun prohibitionists in politics, academia, and the mainstream media, entertainment as well as news, would have us believe that we can trust only government (not ourselves) to protect us (whether from common criminals or terrorists), that only its agents have a right to arms, and that the citizenry has no need to possess the means of opposing government's armed agents or protecting itself from criminals or terrorists. *And note that not even talk-radio conservatives, let alone conservatives in government, have suggested that armed civilians, the real Constitutional militia, be properly trained, organized, and enlisted in the war against terrorism as guards at bridges, water supplies, the border, etc.* Ordinary Americans are encouraged to fight terrorism by continuing to travel and consume—and let's not forget to stock up on duct tape and plastic sheeting.

So as the expiration of the bans on "assault weapons" and detachable magazines holding more than ten rounds approaches, the gun prohibitionists will be out in full force using the sniper rampage, the terrorist threat, and any other tragic event involving the use of weaponry that occurs between now and then to push for making the bans permanent, or even expanding them. And those who support the expiration of the ban will be labeled extremists, if not terrorists themselves, enablers of terrorists. The mainstream media, of course, will assist this demonization of those who dare to point out that the Second Amendment was intended to be the teeth of the Bill of Rights—a defense against tyranny.

It remains to be seen whether the Bush Administration and the Republican-controlled Congress continue to support the Second Amendment or cave in as they did on the "campaign-finance reform" that flew in the face of the First Amendment. The administration has its share of anti-Second Amendment types like Homeland Security head Tom Ridge (who opposed the arming of airline pilots), and they surely will oppose letting the bans expire. And even many who claim to support the Second Amendment tend to qualify that support by stating that the amendment doesn't preclude "reasonable restrictions" on private gun ownership. Solicitor General Theodore Olson has acknowledged the administration's recognition of the individual's right to keep and bear arms even apart from militia membership, but claims that right to be "subject to 'reasonable restrictions' to prevent 'unfit persons' from obtaining firearms and *to limit the possession of some types of weapons that are 'particularly suited to criminal misuse'*" (emphasis added). Given the enlightened conventional wisdom on guns that is completely ignorant of the fact that, as I've described, Americans have until recent decades commonly owned guns with as much or more power and/or firepower than those issued to common soldiers, it may be easy to convince many members of this administration and the Republican-controlled Congress that the "assault weapon" and magazine bans are reasonable. Even conservative talk radio's Second Amendment-supporters are often ignorant concerning guns. Rush Limbaugh once told a caller that there's no such thing as a semiautomatic—guns are either automatic or they aren't. So in order to, say, buy liberal support for a Bush-nominated federal judge, it might seem desirable to give in to an extension on these bans or make them permanent. On the other hand, the bans expire just before the 2004 election, and Democrats as well as Republicans know that anti-gun positions have been hurting politicians while pro-gun positions have been helping them. We shall see.

PART IV

SPOOFING THE GUN PROHIBITIONISTS

HOW ABOUT CAR CONTROL?

Originally published in The New Gun Week, *September 30, 1988.*

Opponents of strict gun laws that aim to restrict drastically or even to prohibit the civilian possession of guns are inclined to argue that "guns don't kill people; people kill people." Proponents of such measures, on the other hand, counter with "people with guns kill people." Well, a small minority of people with guns do that. But people with cars kill and maim many more people annually than do people with guns (car accident fatalities exceed gun fatalities from all causes by some 16,000 or so annually), and even careful drivers pollute our air, use up our precious resources, produce old-car junk for our landscape, require parking lots, and destroy or foul our environment in many other ways. Therefore, if very restrictive gun controls make sense, it would seem that very restrictive car controls make even more sense.

Car controls could be patterned after gun controls that have been proposed, or, in some cases, already enacted. Drivers' licensing requirements would remain the same, but before anyone could buy a car or get a license, he or she would have to have a background check conducted by whichever police agency (local, state, or federal) has been assigned the task of enforcing car controls. A criminal record, a history of emotional, alcohol, or drug problems, and so forth, would automatically disqualify a person for a car permit. But the car permit applicant would not only have to pass such a background check to get his or her permit; he or she would also have to convince the authorities that he or she actually needs a car.

The applicant would have to supply evidence to the authorities to the effect that he or she is physically handicapped but still capable of driving safely, or that he or she lives beyond reasonable walking distance (say one or two miles) from his or her place of employment or school, or from stores carrying basic necessities such as food and clothing, and that bicycles, cars of other family members, city or school buses or other means of public transportation are unavailable or impractical to transport him or her to such places. And the car permit would have to be renewed every year or two, at which time the permit holder would have to verify that he or she still meets the car-ownership requirements or have the permit revoked and give up his or her car. Serious driving violations, criminal convictions, and the like would automatically result in loss of permit, as would proof that the car was being used recreationally (cruising, vacationing, visiting, etc.) or for convenience travel (a trip to the store a couple of blocks away, etc.) by the owner or anyone else.

While such car controls would surely not be greeted with much public support, the media, schools, and properly-worded public opinion polls could be used to propagandize for such measures as these means are often used to propagandize in support of gun controls. And social scientific "research" of the quality until recently typical of that associated with the gun issue would also be useful. Police forces would have to be augmented, of course, but once this is accomplished, the most flagrant violators of car controls would be much easier to spot than are the violators of gun controls. Teenagers driving around after school or parked in shopping center parking lots after store hours would be obvious violators, as would be the owners of most cars parked near nightclubs, taverns, movies, and other such places, and holiday drivers would automatically be suspect. And it should be noted that unlike guns, the ownership of which can be argued to have Constitutional protection, no one claims that the Constitution even remotely protects car possession. Apprehended violators of car controls would simply have their cars confiscated (a significant financial loss); no fines or jail terms would be necessary—the latter provision insuring that jails wouldn't become overcrowded.

Of course, a "car lobby" with much grass-roots, business, and labor support would surely develop, but public-spirited idealists could form a car-control lobby, a Car Control Incorporated, and campaign in behalf of "victims of car violence." A National Coalition to Ban "Speeder Specials" could work to outlaw fast cars (particularly frivolous sports cars) that encourage speeding, though since such cars are often owned by the affluent, such a ban would be even more difficult to achieve than one against the gun controller's favorite target, the cheap "Saturday night special." Perhaps product liability suits would encourage manufacturers to cooperate; after all, attempts have been made to sue handgun manufacturers whose products have been involved in accidents or crimes. Admittedly, other industries (oil, for example) would be less than supportive, but we are dealing with lives and the environment here, and we can't let such interests throw a wrench into the works. Also, new tax-supported jobs would be created as the bureaucracies needed to run this whole program develop—bureaucracies similar to those fostered by gun controls.

Of course, many humane folks who push for gun controls (that don't affect their hobbies and recreations) might not be too enthusiastic about car controls (that would affect their lifestyles). But remember, though quality of life might seem threatened by car controls, actually it should be improved at the same time that lives and the environment are being saved. Social critics often comment on the loss of a sense of community in the United States. Well, with cars no longer available for recreational and convenience use, there is a good probability that neighborhoods would grow up around their own schools, stores, churches, and recreational areas again. And tight-knit neighborhoods should even discourage much of the crime and deviance encouraged by the anonymity associated with the more transient and impersonal nature of large urban settings. Also, more walking and cycling would improve the physical fitness of the general public.

Surely having to rely on public transportation for recreational travel or even to get to work and to shop, inconveniences many people already experience, are no greater than the inconvenience a gunless householder experiences when he or she detects a prowler and must wait for the police to come to his or her rescue. Public transportation, at least, can be developed to the point that schedules are regularly met, but the best police efforts can't ensure that everyone is protected from criminals at all times. And less convenience and recreational driving can be guaranteed to reduce the number of car killings and maimings, since most of these are accidental and less traffic will provide fewer opportunities for accidents—walking into someone or hitting them with a bicycle seldom results in a fatality. Gun victims, on the other hand, are largely criminally- or self-created; therefore, the reduction of the number of guns available, even if this could be accomplished, wouldn't necessarily reduce fatalities, since other weapons, improvised or otherwise, are always available.

Of course, there are many bugs to work out of a car-control scheme, but not too many more than are associated with gun controls. All in all, if very restrictive gun controls make sense, as mentioned previously, very restrictive car controls make even more sense. Somehow, however, I doubt that reformers so willing to risk anything, including civil liberties abuses, to regulate drastically gun possession in the hope that even one life might be saved, would be willing to inconvenience themselves or risk much by drastically regulating car possession. I suspect that while they find it easy to argue that people with guns kill people, they also find it convenient to overlook the fact that people driving cars kill even more people and pollute our environment to boot.

GUNS AND SUPERSTITION: THEN AND NOW

Originally published in The New Gun Week, *June 10, 1988.*

Then

In the middle of the 16th century in part of what is now Germany, the civil and religious authorities came to be concerned about the accuracy of rifles, weapons that had been evolving in central Europe for nearly a century. There was some suspicion that these weapons, with their barrels spiral-grooved (rifled) on the inside, were more accurate than smoothbored muskets because demons were riding their spinning balls and keeping them from straying from the path along which they had been fired. And anything having to do with demons was serious business in 16th-century Europe.

But how could it be determined whether or not demons were joy-riding on rifle balls? Well, while demons would think nothing of riding on a ball made of lead, a base metal if there ever was one, they surely wouldn't come near a bullet made of pure silver, especially if that silver bullet had a crucifix engraved on it. So, being very scientific about the whole business, the authorities had a batch of silver, crucifix-engraved rifle balls made up and had two riflemen, presumably of equal skill, one firing the demon-proof balls, the other using regular lead balls, shoot at a target over two-hundred yards away. Sure enough, the marksman using lead balls hit the target 19 out of 20 times, while the rifleman firing the demon-proof balls didn't hit his mark once. How's that for proof?

A weapon that relied on demons for its effectiveness could not be allowed to exist, of course, so as many rifles as could be found were seized and destroyed, and rifle makers risked being burned at the stake if they continued to produce them. However, this prohibition against rifles was soon forgotten.

Of course, those persons interested in such matters have long since figured out how the spin imparted to a bullet by rifling produces a gyroscopic effect that stabilizes the projectile in its flight and makes its precision placement possible. But why didn't the crucifix-engraved silver bullets fired from a rifle travel as true as the lead bullets? Simple! The rifling tended to strip the silver instead of biting into it as it would with lead, thereby reducing compression, and the engraved crucifix compounded the problem further by throwing the ball out of balance and creating more air turbulence. Gosh, it's nice to live in a scientific-technological age free, at least at the higher intellectual levels, from superstition!

Now

The Members of the National Coalition to Ban handguns (NCBH) want to do exactly what their organization's name implies. Why? Because they believe that handguns are innately troublesome. Josh Sugarmann, NCBH's communication director from 1984 to 1986, spelled out this position in no uncertain terms in the June, 1987 issue of the neoliberal magazine, *The Washington Monthly,* as he criticized another handgun-control organization, Handgun Control Incorporated (HCI). You see, HCI, officially at least, wants to ban only easily concealed short-barreled handguns (a ban that might have to be supplemented by a ban on hacksaws), and tighten restrictions on the acquisition and possession of other types of handguns. But, Sugarmann states, "A 'controlled' handgun kills just as effectively as an 'uncontrolled' one." He continues, "Most control recommendations merely perpetuate the myth that with proper care a handgun can be as safe a tool as any other. Nothing could be further from the truth. A handgun is not a blender."

So the problem is built into handguns themselves; it doesn't arise from the way that some people use such weapons. And Sugarmann cites all sorts of impressive "scientific" support for his and NCBH's claims. Now, the reader will recall that the 16th-century Germans who banned rifles because their bullets were demon-guided also had scientific support. Of course, their scientific test was contaminated by the superstition-infested religion of their day. Not so the scientific support for NCBH's claim that handguns are innately troublesome. The research supporting NCBH's position is permeated by the insights of the 20th-century equivalent of the 16th century Church—the medical establishment. The reader may have noticed that while demons are out of style in modern enlightened circles, disease is in as an explanation for all sorts of troublesome social phenomena.

Citing statistics that indicate that a large percentage of the murders and suicides committed in the United States involve the use of handguns, the Surgeon General's Select Panel for the Promotion of Child Health and the SG's Workshop on Violence and Public Health have both called for a handgun ban (except for the military and police), as has the American Association of Suicidology. And a co-director of the Johns Hopkins Injury Prevention Center sees handguns related to violence as mosquitoes are related to malaria. He argues, "As public health professionals, if we are faced with a disease that is carried by some type of vehicle/vector like a mosquito, our initial response would be to control the vector. There's no reason why if the vehicle/vector is a handgun, we should not be interested in controlling the handgun."

So there we have it! While the rifle was demon-infested in the 16th century, the handgun is a disease carrier in the 20th century. By just being there and handy when someone gets mad at someone else, or gets tired of living and decides to end it all, handguns are responsible for our high murder and suicide rates. But if this is the case, how does one explain why the total number of handgun-related deaths (including justifiable and self-defense homicides, as well as accidents, suicides and criminal homicides) dropped from around 20,000 to under 17,000 annually between 1980 and 1985, according to the FBI Uniform Crime Reports and estimates based on National Center of Health Statistics figures, while the population and number of handguns in circulation increased by 6 and 18 percent respectively during the same period? More people, more handguns (vehicle/vectors), fewer handgun-related deaths! And why do the suicide rates of nations like Japan (20.7), which bans civilian handguns, and Hungary (45.0), which controls them strictly, far exceed the suicide rate in the United States (12.3) where handguns are common? And if, as Sugarmann claims, 40,000,000 of these vehicle/vectors of violence are in circulation in the United States (a very conservative estimate), why is it that even if we accept his inflated figures rather than the 17,000 cited above, handguns are involved in a total of only 22,000 deaths a year? The point isn't that 22,000 is an acceptable number of deaths. The point is that even given the worst-case (and suspect) scenario of the handgun banners, over 99.94 percent of the instruments they wish to ban aren't involved in a life-taking in any given year.

It would seem that where handguns are concerned many moderns who like to think of themselves as enlightened aren't very far removed from 16th-century reasoning.

About the Author

William R. Tonso is a professor emeritus of sociology at the University of Evansville, where his teaching specialties were minority and ethnic group relations, social deviance, social theory, and the sociology of sport. A native of Herrin, Illinois, his Ph.D. in sociology (1976), M.S. in business administration specializing in personnel management (1966), and B.S. in industrial education (1955), are all from Southern Illinois University in nearby Carbondale. Before beginning his 29-year career as a professor, he served as an Air Force officer and worked white collar in industry. He is the author of *Gun and Society: The Social and Existential Roots of the American Attachment to Firearms* and a number of shorter gun-issue pieces published as chapters in books such as Don B. Kates, Jr.'s *Firearms and Violence*, Lee Nisbet's *The Gun Control Debate: You Decide*, and Robert K. Miller's *The Informed Argument*, and in periodicals such as *USA Today*, *The Quill*, *Reason*, *Chronicles*, *Liberty*, *American Rifleman*, *Outdoor Life*, *American Legion*, *Washington Times*, *Cleveland Plain Dealer*, and the *Baltimore Sun*. Dr. Tonso is also the editor of and a contributor to another book, *The Gun Culture* and *Its Enemies*. A member of the National Rifle Association, he lives in Evansville, Indiana with his wife Beverley, two cats, Dexter and Praline, and Cairn Terrier, Caesar.